Cover me in times of war.
A book on faith

Susanne M. Ryan

DEDICATION

To my husband, Steve Ryan: Words will never describe what God did for me when He brought you. You came and messed up my way of thinking and believing. It was uncomfortable until I realized you have a level of faith I didn't understand and hadn't obtained. You thought out of the box I had put God in, and He used you to bring clarity to my mess.

Thank you for living your life out loud with nothing hidden from anyone. Your honesty makes people realize that there are others just like them.

I see Jesus in you, and so do others. I love you forever.

To my Dad: Thanks for being an example of strength from the first time you sat me on the counter at five years old to pray the sinner's prayer, buying me my favorite and first 'grown-up' Bible and to the first time you called yourself the F.B.I. *(Father Being Involved)*. You taught me how to shoot my first bow and arrow, fire a weapon, quietly follow you on a hunting trail, and even learned to love the '3 Stooges' on a Sunday after church.

Most of all, thank you for always being there in the good, the bad, and the ugly. The legacy that you and mom will someday leave behind will be left for many generations to come. Thank you for being you.

CONTENTS

ACKNOWLEDGMENTS

This book is for all the preachers, pastors, teachers, mentors, and Christians who speak a word in due season. Some of the knowledge I have of the Bible comes from my research and study. Still, insight, creativity, and understanding also come from the great people around me, including those I may listen to and will never know personally. Thanks to them for all their laboring to share the Gospel with people like myself!

To Joe Kuchinski:
I added a few pictures and blank pages for your coloring pleasure, as you requested. =)

Psalm 140:7 says,
"O God the Lord, the strength of my salvation,
You have covered my head in the day of battle."

COVER ME IN TIMES OF WAR

1. COVER ME

Life is a battle. There is always something challenging to choose from: finances, sickness, jobs, relationships, family, . . . We must believe we will go for a win in challenges. Something must rise and challenge things around us. Too much of our time is spent living by the rules of a kingdom that we are not a part of. I don't want to live by the rules that are not for my life. We can find out if we are living by the right standards by answering questions like: Does that fit what God says about me? Is that what I believe about my God?

If I need a pay raise and there are no pay raises, then the rules need to change. God said He would prosper me, so something needs change. No jobs, but I need one? I either believe what everyone else is saying about no work available, or I know that God has rules that are bigger than my circumstances. The way God operates needs to be bigger than the way I think. Whose rules are we fighting and living under? The world's rules or God's rules? Too many times, I have tried to do God's fighting for Him. When I do God's fighting for Him, I get in the way. God is the one who wants to fight on our behalf. He

3

does a much better job of being God than I could ever do.

Psalm 140:7 says, *"O God the Lord, the strength of my salvation. You have covered my head in the day of battle."* David knew that no matter what weapons he may possess, the greatest protection was God Himself! This is why he was able to go against Goliath with a sling and some stones. He knew that if he would do his part and be faithful and diligent, God would do His part and make up the rest.

Let's look at what has happened to this point that David says, "Cover my head in the day of battle." This is the Susanne Ryan Bible Recap Version: Israel has complained to God about wanting a king, so God complies and gives them Saul. Saul worked out for a while, but Saul did not always do things the way God commanded. Samuel, the prophet, tells King Saul that because of his actions of disobedience, God has taken the throne away from Saul and his household. Samuel is sent to the house of Jesse, where after meeting all of Jesse's sons (7 of them), God tells him to bring the youngest son, David, who was tending sheep. Samuel anoints David and says that he will be the next king of Israel. God departs King Saul, and now Saul is left in distress.

Have you ever tried to live without God? It's rough; it is Godless. If God is good and you are living without God, then you are living without anything good. That's rough, and I don't recommend trying this!

Saul is so distressed that he asks his servants to provide someone who can play an instrument. Somebody speaks up and says that they know this son of Jesse, who can play the harp. Go figure. They mention the guy who had been previously anointed to take King Saul's spot.

1 Samuel 16:18,

> *"Then one of the servants answered and said, "Look, I have seen a son of Jesse the Bethlehemite, who is skillful in playing, a mighty man of valor, a man of war, prudent in speech, and a handsome person; and the Lord is with him."*

In the middle of doing life, David was anointed king and then sent back to the sheep. "You shall be king over Israel! Now go back to the field." Huh. That's not how I would like it to play out. My version would have been something like this: "You shall be king over Israel! Here are your enormous and gleaming crown and scepter. We will have a parade, and you shall ride the finest camel in all the lands! We shall announce to everyone we pass that you are now king over all the land! You will eat what you want, sleep where you want, and everyone will be at your beck and call!" *That is more like it.* But no, he went back to the smelly, stinky, and dirty sheep.

In his ordinary life, God prepared him for battle as a king. It doesn't say how long after he was anointed that he ended up before Saul, but by the time he appears before Saul, he has grown because Saul makes him his armor-bearer.

1 Samuel 16:19-21,

> *"Therefore, Saul sent messengers to Jesse, and said, "Send me*
> *your son David, who is with the sheep." And Jesse took a donkey loaded*
> *with bread, a skin of wine, and a young goat, and sent them by his son*
> *David to Saul. So, David came to Saul and stood before him. And he*
> *loved him greatly, and he became his armorbearer."*

We know from the Bible that David still must have helped his father with sheep because, by the time we get to the story of David and Goliath, we see that David's father sends him from the sheep to his brothers who are on the battle line.

On one side of a broad valley are the Philistine's and the other side stands Israel. The battle is as such: each army sends out their best warrior, and the winner takes all. Philistines send out Goliath, the giant. Israel sends no one; 40 days and 40 nights. All-day long, Goliath taunts Israel, and they are in a standoff. Every day Goliath returns to the valley, but Israel has no one to send on their behalf.

Up to this point in history, there have been many miracles for Israel. They have escaped from Pharaoh in Egypt, the Red Sea parted, cloud by day and fire by night, water from a rock, manna from heaven, the Promised Land, another parting of the Red Sea, the walls of Jericho have fallen! There are so many times that God stepped in and took over, and yet, here is Israel dismayed and scared that they may lose.

1 Samuel 17:16-26,

"And the Philistine drew near and presented himself forty days, morning and evening. Then Jesse said to his son David, "Take now for your brothers an ephah of this dried grain and these ten loaves and run to your brothers at the camp. And carry these ten cheeses to the captain of their thousand, and see how your brothers fare and bring back news of them.

So, David rose early in the morning, left the sheep with a keeper, and took the things and went as Jesse had commanded him. And he came to the camp as the army was going out to the fight and shouting for the battle. For Israel and the Philistines had drawn up in battle array, army against army.

Then as he talked with them, there was the champion, the Philistine of Gath, Goliath by name, coming up from the armies of the Philistines; and he spoke according to the same words. So, David heard them. And all the men of Israel said, "Have you seen this man who has come up? Surely, he has come up to defy Israel; and it shall be that the man who kills him the king will enrich with great riches, will give him his daughter, and give his father's house exemption from taxes in Israel.

*Then David spoke to the men who stood by him, saying, "What shall be done for the man who kills the Philistine and takes away the reproach from Israel? For who is this uncircumcised Philistine, that he should defy the armies of the **living God**?"*

David had confidence that no other man in Israel had: OUR GOD IS ALIVE.

1 Samuel 17:28-39,

Now Eliab his oldest brother heard when he spoke to the men; and Eliab's anger was aroused against David, and he said, "Why did you come down here? And with whom have you left those few sheep in the wilderness? I know your pride and the insolence of your heart, for you have come down to see the battle.

And David said, "What have I done now? Is there not a cause?" Then he turned from him toward another and said the same thing, and these people answered him as the first ones did.

Now when the words which David spoke were heard, they reported them to Saul; and he sent for him. Then David said to Saul, "Let no man's heart fail because of him; your servant will go and fight with this Philistine." And Saul said to David, "You are not able to go against this Philistine to fight with him; for you are a youth, and he a man of war from his youth." But David said to Saul, "Your servant used to keep his father's sheep, and when a lion or a bear came and took a lamb out of the flock, I went out after it and struck it, and delivered the lamb from its mouth; and when it arose against me, I caught it by its beard, and struck and killed it. Your servant has killed both lion and bear; and this uncircumcised Philistine will be like one of them, seeing he has defied the armies of the living God."

Moreover, David said, "The Lord, who delivered me from the paw of the lion and the paw of the bear. He will deliver me from the hand of the Philistine." And Saul said to David, "Go, and the Lord be with you!

So, Saul clothed David with his armor, and he put a bronze helmet on his head; he also clothed him with a coat of mail. David fastened his sword to his armor and tried to walk, for he had not tested them. And David said to Saul, "I cannot walk with these, for I have not tested them." So, David took them off."

David knew his strength was not the strength of the others. His power didn't come from the same source. If even Saul could not wear his armor and fight the giant, how and why would David, not ever having worn the armor before, be able to fight?

Cover me in time of war.

David knew that it wasn't about winning for Saul or even for his fame; he knew that they would win because God was his covering. God made up for what David lacked, and if David remembered that God was the source, he would be alright.

1 Samuel 17:45-47,

"Then David said to the Philistine, "You come to me with a sword, with a spear, and with a javelin. But I come to you in the name of the Lord of hosts, the God of the armies of Israel, whom you have defiled. This day the Lord will deliver you into my hand, and I will strike you and take your head from you. And this day I will give the carcasses of

the camp of the Philistines to the birds of the air and the wild beasts of the earth, that all the earth may know that there is a God in Israel. Then all this assembly shall know that the Lord does not save with sword and spear; for the battle is the Lord's, and He will give you into our hands."

David knew that all glory, for any battle, belonged to the Lord. Without God, as the covering, there would be no win. The army spent forty days talking to each other about who couldn't beat Goliath. David arrived fresh from the field, fresh from God believing and knowing that God could beat anybody and anything. He had no idea Goliath was unbeatable. Even when they told him, he didn't believe it. What he thought about God was so above anything about the circumstance that he couldn't understand why no one was going down to kill him and come back again! David was caught up with God and God's rules and God's ways of thinking.

God is saying, "I am the King of this kingdom, and you are my subjects. Where I am the King of the kingdom, it is My rules. My rules about sickness, relationships, finances, church, and how things should grow and thrive. Let's play by My rules and not the world's rules and ways."

We can sit back and say that we are in a global financial crisis, there are no jobs, no promotions, no starting a business, wrong time for this or that, don't sell your house, sell your house. I think God must sit back on His throne and wonder who made up our rules. Who said this is the wrong time to do that? Whose word overcomes His Word? Whose words are more powerful than His words?

God is looking for people who say they are ready to break the rules of the kingdoms of this world; a people who are prepared to turn things around and who are not going to live by the world anymore. Israel stood on a hillside and looked at Goliath and saw his size and height and how intimidating and unbeatable he was. David stood on a hill and looked at the giant and saw how much smaller Goliath was than David's God. A ten-foot giant is no comparison to the God of the Universe!

I learned at a young age that having Jesus as my best friend was better than anyone else. God never lets me down; He always tells the truth, looks out for me, is there whenever I call Him. He is my confidant, I say my deepest secrets to Him, and He never laughs at me or mocks me. When people base their whole life on happiness that comes from popularity, then when your popularity goes away, or your friends are out of town, you are alone.

Despite all the problems we may feel, we can be best friends with Jesus. The Creator of the Universe, the one who hung the moon and stars and called them all by name, the God who knows how many hairs are on my head, how many nights I have laid awake worrying, the fear I may feel, the personal struggles I have – Jesus becomes my source of everything.

When you get to know God on a personal level rather than just a God who is out there that made creation, you begin to understand that you can do anything because He is with you. He knows your heart, and you can know His. David knew who he was because he knew who

HE was.

Those around him did not see David as someone who could do battle, think wisely, get involved in the affairs of other men, let alone on behalf of a whole nation. Yet, David was willing not to have a fear of man, fear of the opinion of man, and instead, he took on what he knew God said about him.

Who I am is not who **I think I am**, but who **God says I am**. I am so far from who God intended me to be, but when I put myself in the hands and care of God, He makes up for what I am not. It is in Him that I become complete.

You are created for a purpose. You have been fearfully and wonderfully made, which means that God has a plan for you. If you don't know exactly what that plan is, I am here to tell you! **MAKE HIS NAME KNOWN!** Show others that your God is the most powerful. Point all you do to Jesus.

Cover me in the day of war. David had no physical covering, but he knew God was all he needed.

Psalm 23,

> *"The Lord is my shepherd; I shall not want. He makes me to lie down in green pastures; He leads me beside the still waters. He restores my soul; He leads me in the paths of righteousness for His name's sake. Yea, though I walk through the valley of the shadow of death, I will fear no evil; for You are with me; Your rod and Your staff, they comfort me.*

You prepare a table before me in the presence of my enemies; You anoint my head with oil; My cup runs over. Surely goodness and mercy shall follow me all the days of my life, and I will dwell in the house of the Lord forever."

He prepares a table before me in the presence of my enemies! That means that He makes an eight-course meal, a banqueting table is set out, a long, drawn-out, satisfying meal. That meal is in the middle of battle, war is all around me, and there I sit at my meal that He has prepared in peace. War rages on and all the while David says, **Cover me in time of war**.

"God! When I don't understand what is going on, I have a peace that surpasses all my understanding, and I have a joy that is my strength. When all hell is breaking loose around me, I have confidence that God is my covering!"

Revelations 4:11,

"You are worthy, our Lord and God, to receive glory and honor and power, for you created all things, and by Your will, they were created and have their being."

May He cover you in times of war!

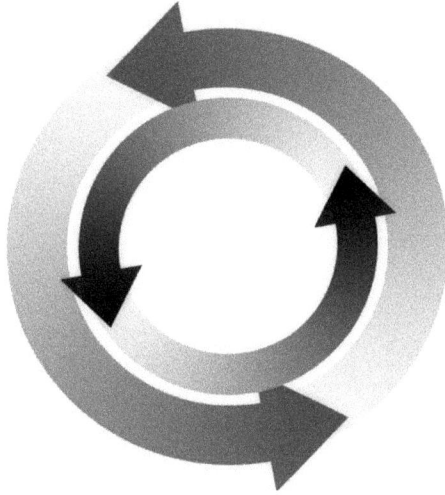

Romans 7:15,
*"I do the things I don't want to do
and I don't do the things I want to do."*

2. CYCLEPATH

Have you ever been at a point in your life where the scenery seems the same? You're on a path you know you have been before, or maybe you find yourself in situations that always look the same? That's called a Cyclepath. I made up a new term.

A Cyclepath is someone who, not to be confused with a psychopath, finds themselves on a hamster wheel of life. It is the same kind of scenario over and over; you respond the same way, you act the same way, you have the same type of friends and relationships. You thought you learned before, but now you realize you didn't learn, you just recognized the path and went at it again. You're a Cyclepath.

In the 1990s, our church went through a revival of sorts. How many know that dessert can be good, but if you're not taught to eat right, then eventually, the dessert just becomes unhealthy. If we fill our altars and people are healed and delivered, but we never teach them and disciple them in the things of God, then they will always return to the altar for the same things. They will never learn to get out of their rut, out of their cycle that took them to the rut in the first place.

During this time, I had a dream. I don't know about you, but it isn't often I remember my dreams, so when I do, I know I need to take notes. I think God knows I need all the beauty sleep I can get!

I was walking up this huge, beautiful mountain. We went day by day climbing. We had a few stops where we would unload our backpacks and rest, but we always kept moving. It seemed like every time we stopped; a few items were left from our backpacks because they became heavier and heavier as we ascended. It wasn't bad that we left things since they seemed to be things that we didn't need, but for some reason, we had packed.

Days into our journey, we reached an outlook on the mountain path. It was beautiful. There was a stream with fresh, cold water, and although the path led there, I could see that it also kept moving forward. We made a warm campfire and rested for the night.

The next morning, I awoke to pick up my belongings to begin our travel. For some reason, I had an urgency to hurry up and get moving on our journey. But as I walked around camp, I realized that many hadn't planned to move on. They wouldn't listen even when I reminded them that our goal was to reach the top of the mountain. In fact, they started to make plans to build a small city here and raise their families.

When I woke up from the dream, I asked God what this meant. It was then that I realized that there are places in our journey that we are refreshed and comforted, but some people stop at the point in their lives that God didn't mean for them to stop. They made their home in what is intended to be a season. They settled for a view of the valley when they should've moved on and reached the top of the mountain. It was the top of the mountain where they could take all of creation in and the glory of God in wholeness.

We tend to stop when we get comfortable. We settle for good but not God. We make an altar around emotion to music; we try to bottle up the personal ministry, and we crave a word from a prophet when God has supplied a whole book of His words. And thus, we begin our life as a Cyclepath.

What better person to learn from in the Bible about being a Cyclepath than Jacob? He was a classic Cyclepath, and by the end of his life, he finally learned his lesson. We first hear about him when he is not even born. He had already started his life as a Cyclepath while yet in his mother's womb!

Genesis 25:22-26 says,

> *"But the children struggled together within her; and she said, "If all is well, why am I like this?" So, she went to inquire of the Lord. And the Lord said to her: "Two nations are in your womb, two peoples shall be separated from your body; one people shall be stronger than the other, and the older shall serve the younger." So, when her days were fulfilled for her to give birth, indeed, there were twins in her womb. And the first came out red. He was like a hairy garment all over; so, they called his name Esau. Afterward, his brother came out, and his hand took hold of Esau's heel; so, his name was called Jacob. Isaac was sixty years old when she bore them."*

Esau was born very hairy and red; thus, his name means just that. Jacob's name means supplanter or schemer, someone who gains because of trickery or a deceiver. How's that for a lifetime label?

In Jacob's time, a father would leave the bulk of their inheritance to the eldest son of the family. They would pray a blessing over their children when they knew they were old and dying. They would bless all their children, but a special blessing and inheritance would fall on the eldest son. Once a blessing was given and prayed, it could not be taken back. Blessings were not "well-wishing"; they were more of a prophecy.

I have always heard the story of Jacob and Esau and assumed they were dueling, young brothers, maybe in their teens or early 20's. However, when you look at a timeline, you can see that they are not young, but in their 70's! Technically, that makes Jacob a scheming older man!

The Bible says that the boys grew old, and Esau was a skillful hunter, a man of the field. Jacob dwelt in the tents and was mild-mannered. Esau could kill game, and he was considered strong; Jacob would take the game and make stew and cook; one had a bow and an arrow; the other had a pan. Their father, Isaac, loved Esau because he was the oldest and could hunt, and he ate what he killed. Jacob was loved by his mother, Rebekah, and was what we would consider a "momma's boy."

One day, Esau is out hunting and comes home exhausted. Have you ever been so exhausted that you were willing to do almost anything? He was exhausted. He comes back to find Jacob and asks

Jacob to make his famous stew. Jacob, knowing Esau's weakness for food and his desperation, decided to do what siblings do; he bargained for a blessing and inheritance.

Genesis 25:29-34 says,

> *"Now Jacob cooked a stew, and Esau came in from the field, and he was weary. And Esau said to Jacob, "Please feed me with that same red stew, for I am weary." Therefore, his name was called Edom. But Jacob said, "Sell me your birthright as of this day." And Esau said, "Look, I am about to die; so, what is this birthright to me?" Then Jacob said, "Swear to me as of this day." So, he swore to him and sold his birthright to Jacob. And Jacob gave Esau bread and stew of lentils; then he ate and drank, arose, and went his way. Thus, Esau despised his birthright."*

Years later, we find that their father, Isaac, is about to die. He calls his eldest son Esau and tells him to go and hunt game, prepare a meal and bring it to him that he can now bless him. Esau has an opportunity to admit to his father that he has sold his inheritance years before, but he doesn't. He goes out as his father asks and hunts.

Rebekah, his wife, heard the conversation and went to Jacob. She tells him that he deserves the birthright and inheritance and derives a plan to trick Isaac into blessing Jacob instead.

Genesis 27:18-24,

> *"So, he went to his father and said, "My father." And he said,*

"Here I am. Who are you, my son?" Jacob said to his father, "I am Esau your firstborn; I have done just as you told me; please arise, sit and eat of my game, that your soul may bless me." But Isaac said to his son, "How is it that you have found it so quickly, my son?" And he said, "Because the Lord your God brought it to me." Isaac said to Jacob, "Please come near, that I may feel you, my son, whether you are really my son Esau or not." So, Jacob went near to Isaac, his father, and he felt him and said, "The voice is Jacob's voice, but the hands are the hands of Esau." And he did not recognize him, because his hands were hairy like his brother Esau's hands; so, he blessed him. Then he said, "Are you really my son Esau?" he said, "I am."

I find it very interesting that in verse 20 when Isaac asks how it was that he could hunt and kill the game so quickly, Jacob's response was, "Because the Lord your God brought it to me." You can see that at this point in Jacob's life, God is not his God but his father's God. His father's God has not been made real in his life yet.

Isaac blesses Jacob thinking he is Esau. By the time Esau returns, they realize what Jacob has done, and a new wedge is put in place between the brothers. It wasn't long before Jacob runs from Esau, knowing that he will kill him if he gets the chance. As you read the story of Jacob, you find that just as he is a schemer, so are others around him. What he has done in his own life has also been attracted to his life.

Jacob wants to marry Rachel but is tricked into marrying the sister, Leah. Eventually, he marries the woman he loved, but trickery was never far from his life; deceit was always around the corner.

One day, Jacob hears that his brother Esau is coming to meet with him. Not only is he coming to meet with him, but Esau is bringing 400 men with him. That's a bad day; that's a "dark alley" moment. It doesn't look good for Jacob, and his past is catching up with him quickly. He sends servants with a multitude of presents to give to his brother and appease the anger he remembers that Esau had. He wakes in the middle of the night and sends his family across the brook while he decides to stay on the other side. He knows something must change, and he doesn't know if it will be good or bad.

Genesis 32:22-30,

> *"And he arose that night and took his two wives, his two female servants, and his eleven sons, and crossed over the ford of Jabbok. He took them, sent them over the brook, and sent over what he had. Then Jacob was left alone, and a Man wrestled with him until the breaking of the day. Now when He saw that He did not prevail against him, He touched the socket of his hip; and the socket of Jacob's his was out of joint as He wrestled with him."*

Jacob is no longer a young man. They estimate that he could have very well been around 97 years old at this point. The fact that his hip was out of place can happen as an older man; however, what was unusual for Jacob was the fact that he was in the same position he was earlier in life. We first hear about Jacob in the womb, he grabbed his brother's heel. Then we hear about him again, and he has tricked his father and seized the blessing, stolen the blessing of his brother. Now he is wrestling with God.

This is a cycle in his life. Have you ever been in a cycle? "Why do I do what I don't want to do?" Sometimes we do things we don't want to do because it is familiar, and that is just the "way we do it." It is a habit, and we don't even think about it. Even Paul said in Romans 7, *"I do the things I don't want to do, and I don't do the things I want to do."* It is a cycle. The path you are on is a cycle; you have been here before, and you're in a rut! Jacob finds himself in this spot. He is wrestling once again for what he wants.

Genesis 32:26-30,

> *"And He said, "Let Me go, for the day breaks." But he said, "I will not let You go unless You bless me!" So, He said to him, "What is your name?" He said, "Jacob." And He said, "Your name shall no longer be called Jacob, but Israel; for you have struggled with God and with men, and have prevailed." Then Jacob asked, saying, "Tell me Your name, I pray." And He said, "Why is it that you ask My name?" And He blessed him there. So, Jacob called the name of the place Peniel: "For I have seen God face to face, and my life is preserved."*

He has an opportunity for a do-over! He was asked by his father when he was younger, "What is your name?" and he lied and said it was Esau. From that lie, he deceived and stole the blessing; he lived all these years on a blessing that didn't truly belong to him. So, here is his do-ver.

"What is your name?" said the man.

"This is a fine time to get acquainted. You've broken my hip, and now you want to know who I am? Jacob. My name is Jacob. I am the deceiver. I am the liar, backstabber, heel grabber. I am the one who always wants to be first. I am the stealer of blessings. My name is Jacob. Bless me. I am Jacob."

THAT is when he was blessed. We serve a God of compassion and mercy. Instead of looking at Jacob's past, He looks at Jacob's future. Jacob grabs his brother's heel in the womb and is thus named deceiver, but now he wrestles again and tells the truth. Now he is renamed Israel, prevailer. His tenacity has overcome his deceit. His desire for a true blessing has made him wrestle harder and stronger. He is tired of the cycle and repetition. He tells the truth.

Why didn't the man he wrestled with tell him his name when Jacob asked? Verse 29, *"Tell me your name, I pray."* And He said, *"Why is it that you ask about My name?"*. And He blessed him there." Sometimes God doesn't show up to tell you about Himself; He shows up to tell you about who you are in Him. He didn't need Jacob to know more about God. He needed Jacob to know who he was **in** God. He has always wrestled with others, but now someone is wrestling with him.

Genesis 32:26, *"Let me go for it is daybreak."* Jacob said, *"I will not let You go unless You bless me."* You have found God when you hold on to God even when it would be easier to let go! He had a tenacity; the same one that worked against him all those years now works for him. He might be hurting, old, lost some time, but he didn't let go.

Occasionally you must decide in your life that you want something bad enough. You're sick of pretending and posing. You have to stand up and say, "I will not let You go unless You bless me! I have been holding on to heels all my life, but now I'm holding on to the only one who has the power to bless me."

The angel says *(Susanne Ryan Bible Version)*, "I see who you pretended to be, but who are you?"

Jacob says, "Okay, I'm out here on my own, and I'm ready to take off Esau's clothes. I'm ready to let go of heels and be myself. I will tell you who I am. I struggle; I have some issues. I'm Jacob."

Then the man said, "Your name will no longer be Jacob but Israel."

Once he admits his real name, God gives him a new one. "Because you have struggled." <u>You see, it isn't always in your success, but in your struggle that God will show you who you are.</u> You have struggled with God and man and overcome.

Aren't you glad He gives us a new name? He doesn't call you what you did or who you were: adulterer, murderer, liar, cheat, depressed, sad, lonely, or weak. He calls you beloved; He calls you loved, blessed, righteous, holy, and pure. Jacob not only got a new name but a new identity!

Israel means triumphant with God. "Jacob is who I am, and Israel is who He is in me!" From this point forward, I would expect they would call him by his new name, Israel. Occasionally he is called Jacob, and sometimes he is referred to as Israel. Why give a new name if he isn't going to use it all the time? Just because he had a new name didn't mean he wasn't going to have struggles. It is a process. Sometimes God may call you Israel, but you still feel like a Jacob. The good news is that God is not conflicted by your inadequacies!

Many years later, in Exodus 3:15, we read that Jacob is dead. The Israelites that came through is family are enslaved in Egypt, and God appears to a man named Moses. Moses asks God the same thing Jacob asked God. "Who are you? Suppose I go to the Egyptians, and they ask who sent me. Who do I say you are?"

God replies, "I Am. Say that I Am sent you."

"I am the God of Abraham. I am the God of Isaac. I am the God of Jacob."

If I were God, I would want to be the God of their good sides! I would say, "I am the God of Abraham, Isaac, and Israel. I am the God of the guy that was changed in a wrestling match."

But instead, He says to Moses and us today,

"If you want to know who I am, I am the God of Jacob. I am the God of that part of you that you don't want anyone else to see or talk about. I am not just the God of your success but the God of your struggles. I am the God of your

victories and the God of your defeats. I am the God of Jacob."

It is comforting to know that our God is full of mercy, grace, and truth. No matter how long we have been a Cyclepath, He is still our God.

UNQUALIFIED

Matthew 28:18-20,

> *"Then Jesus came and spoke to them, saying, "All authority has been given to Me in heaven and on earth. 'Go, therefore, and make disciples of all the nations, baptizing them in the name of the Father and of the Son and of the Holy Spirit, teaching them to observe all things that I have commanded you; and lo, I am with you always, even to the end of the age."*

COVER ME IN TIMES OF WAR

3. UNQUALIFIED

Have you ever been unqualified for something? Maybe a new job, a loan of some kind, a higher education? When you apply for a home loan, you get "qualified" for a specific amount based on who you are, your history, and what you have. Have you ever felt unqualified to do what you know that God has asked you to do?

I often have found myself thinking things like: They can pray better than I can. They can lay hands on someone, and people will be healed. They know the "formula" to make sure that God will move. They know how to worship right, pray right, move right, say the right thing, or do the right thing. THEY! THEY! THEY!

Matthew 28:18-20,

> "Then Jesus came and spoke to them, saying, "All authority has been given to Me in heaven and on earth. 'Go, therefore, and make disciples of all the nations, baptizing them in the name of the Father and of the Son and of the Holy Spirit, teaching them to observe all things that I have commanded you; and lo, I am with you always, even to the end of the age."

Those verses in Matthew are what we call the Great

Commission. Jesus said this to all believers in the Bible. It is a commission that Jesus gave to each of us. It is a job we have been given, but most times we think that we are not qualified to be the one to carry out this commission. The pastor is qualified, the guest speaker is qualified, someone who has been saved longer.

We live in a world today that is in division. Turn the news on, and the division between black and white is loud and clear, Democrat and Republican, man and woman. You will have a hard time finding people who see eye to eye these days. One thing that unites Christians, no matter what color, country, man or woman, is our mission and commission that we have been given.

David Livingston said, *"Forbid that we should ever consider a commission from the King of kings a sacrifice so long as men esteem the role of an earthly government as an honor."* This statement, although it was said over 150 years ago, is true today. We have people who think a role in the world is much greater than any call by God. This can't be further from the truth.

A few years back, I went to a Christian summer camp with my then eight-year-old daughter. She was so excited. I saved money all year to pay for us to go, and because she was so young, I had to sign up as a camp counselor. It was a long week. A whole week is a long time when you're eight years old and have only been away for a day or two; a full week is a long time for a mom to oversee eight other little girls.

I had girls in my cabin between the ages of eight and twelve years old. They were from all different backgrounds and all different life stories, from foster care, pastors' kids to never been in church. I felt completely unqualified for this job. I have two of my own kids, but I certainly don't have eight of them from all different backgrounds.

On the last night, we were given items to do communion together with our cabin. So, the last night I took them all out to a field that had some seats and bleachers. We all brought a notebook and our Bibles. I explained, in kid terms, why we take communion and could tell quickly they were all lost on the subject. One little girl said bluntly that she had "heard of this thing before," but just thought it was a grownup thing.

I asked them all if they thought that God could heal. Some said yes, some said they believe when we pray, but it doesn't do anything. My unqualification felt very real at this point. Adults can be polite, but kids demand an answer.

Another little girl asked why it was a big deal to know God and this stuff. I thought for sure that I was going to have a God moment with them until she went all ADD and looked at the moon and shouted, "Wow! Look how bright it is tonight! That is so cool!" In frustration at having to reign back the eight little girls to the conversation, I realized again I was very unqualified.

Finally, I asked how many knew Jesus personally. A few of them looked at me oddly. I said again, "Do you know Jesus? Do you remember a time that you met Him?" Some told me how they prayed the sinner's prayer; one told me she didn't understand God's stuff, and another told me how she had been baptized as a baby.

I stood up and pointed to the sky. "Do you see that moon? The one you said was so bright? The creator of the world made that!" They all giggled.

I pointed at the one little girl that had given me so many disciplinary problems that week and I said, "Destiny, that same creator of the world is waiting to know you!" She giggled again. I felt unqualified.

Turning to another little girl, I said, "Katie, those stars right there that hang in the sky, the ones that don't ever fall, the ones that are bright up there?" I pointed in the direction of the brightest area and paused to get them all to listen and look. "The same God that created those stars is waiting to talk to you." She giggled, and again I felt unqualified.

Our conversation finally turned back to communion. We wrote prayer requests, and we took communion. ...they giggled the whole time... I felt even more unqualified.

Inside my head, the conversation went something like this: "What am I doing here!? Why did I think I could connect with these kids? What makes me qualified to do so!?" I was frustrated.

Finally, we stood in a circle, and I told them we were all going to pray for one another. We all read our prayer request out loud and then took hands to begin praying. I thought for sure this is where the God moment would take place. I started the prayer, and the girl next to me went next. We got about three or four girls into praying when suddenly someone let loose the loudest fart ever. It was loud. There was no denying it. The forest was dark and quiet, and the silence broke. The giggles started again, and although I may have giggled as well, I felt so unqualified. I couldn't even get through prayer with these girls!

That's when I realized we are all unqualified. It isn't about talking right or making a good point to someone else. It is about pointing people to Jesus. I can never learn enough or do enough to be qualified. The thing that makes me qualified is the fact that I have Jesus. It is the fact that I must be willing to share Jesus with someone who may not understand.

I shared Jesus with the girls; some got it, and some didn't, but I shared Him. I would make them stop when someone got hurt and pray. They had some odd looks the first time, but by the second time, they were pros!

I found them holding out their hands to the one who got hurt or was sick. We laid hands on the sick, and we prayed. We prayed for Katie, who was very homesick, we prayed for Lucy who had hurt her knee, we prayed for Helaina who got sun poisoning on the first day there. We were qualified. I made sure they all knew that when they went home, they could still pray. Katie, of course, wanted to make sure it would work on all her pets at home too. I assured her that was the case.

You see, a disciple in Jesus' time would have to learn the first five books of the Bible, word for word, by the age of five or six. The whole Old Testament had to be memorized by the age of twelve. They would then find a Rabbi and ask to follow him. The goal was to be just like the Rabbi and do precisely what the Rabbi did.

The Rabbi, in turn, no doubt, quiz and test the student to see if the student truly had learned and memorized the whole Old Testament – word for word. If the student passed, the Rabbi would tell the student that he was qualified and could follow him; he would be his Rabbi and teach him all he knows so the student would become just like him. The student would drop everything and follow the Rabbi who had accepted him. If a student failed to learn the Old Testament, they would find a different job; a fisherman, tent maker, merchant, tax collector, shepherd, etc.

Jesus was called Rabbi or Teacher. The disciples did not go to Jesus, but Jesus went to the disciples. Jesus didn't follow the protocol of the other Rabbi's. A disciple was supposed to go to the Rabbi, not the Rabbi, to the disciple. Jesus wanted them to follow Him; He wanted to teach them so they could, in turn, be more like Him.

He went to them and said, "Come follow Me." They were not scholars; they were fishermen and market place people. They were not the cream of the crop or the top of their class. They couldn't make it and couldn't pass; they weren't good enough to follow a Rabbi. They had found another job, and yet Jesus said, "Come follow Me," and they dropped everything.

Where is the test? Jesus didn't give them a test to see if they knew the Bible in whole. There was no test. Jesus pointed and told them to follow. A Rabbi would only tell students that he believed could do what he did to follow him. When Jesus said, "Come follow Me," He was saying, "You can be like me. You can do what I do." Jesus was taking a bunch of guys who had flunked out of school, and he chooses them based on their potential – not their qualifications. They dropped it all to do and be like their Rabbi.

Jesus did the opposite of the world; He messed up the normal. The student was supposed to pursue the Rabbi, not the Rabbi pursue the student. Therefore, the other Rabbis were so upset when someone would call Jesus 'Teacher or Rabbi'. They were shocked when Jesus would make a new disciple because He was picking people that the others had turned down! He was picking those who were not qualified for the job.

We find the famous story of Peter walking on water in Matthew 14. The waves are crashing all around, and the wind is blowing strong. The disciples look out and see His figure on the water, and it says that they were terrified and feared it was a ghost. Jesus tells them to take courage and not be afraid. But Peter! I love this guy! He calls out to Jesus and says, "Lord, if it is, you tell me to come to you on the water." Jesus says, "Come."

Peter knew that if it was indeed Jesus and He told him to come then, that would mean Peter could go. He knew his Rabbi would only ask him to do what He believed Peter could do. Once Jesus told him to come out, Peter had no doubt he could do it. His Rabbi had called him!

Peter walks out on the water and falls. Jesus says, "You of little faith! Why do you doubt?" Is Peter doubting Jesus? No. He doubts himself! Jesus was telling him he could do it because He wouldn't have called him if He didn't believe he could! "I would have never chosen you if I didn't think you could do it!"

Jesus' last commandment is to go and make more disciples. "Go and do what I have done with you. Choose them and tell them they can do it because your Rabbi could do it, and now you can do it!" Jesus took a bunch of nobodies and told them they were somebody! He took the unqualified and made them qualified.

God not only rescues us from where we are, but He chooses us because He believes we can do what He does. Jesus says, "You didn't choose me, but I choose you. I called you and told you to come. Leave it all behind. Take the baggage off. I have told you it is okay. You are qualified because I am qualified."

Jesus told the rich young ruler to sell it all and follow Him. Jesus tells the fishermen to cast their nets, and they will get fish. They get fish, but it never says they cashed in on their big catch! They left it all and followed Him.

We all lug around baggage, but God is telling us to follow Him without anything else. Leave it all behind. Don't count on the stuff that weighs you down. Some of us have all sorts of baggage, holding us back and making us feel even more unqualified.

You've heard the saying, "He's carrying a lot of baggage from his past!" or "Avoid her, she's got so much baggage!" Did you know that the word baggage comes from the word 'luggage'? It means to 'lug' something around.

We get baggage from other people by the things they do to us or the things they say to us. If we carry those things around, we carry baggage. We begin collecting baggage when we're just little kids.

I use to stutter as a kid, and it made me feel stupid at a young age. I heard a baby sitter once tell a friend that she thought it was funny that I said my 'R' as a 'W.' The word "Red" was "Wed" and "Round" was "Wound."

It's all funny until it's YOUR funny! You've heard the saying, "Sticks and stones may break my bones, but words will never hurt me." Well, guess what? It's one of the biggest lies that you've ever been taught. Words can cut so deep, and if we don't learn to let go of those wounds, and realize who we are in Christ, what we do is pick up more baggage and carry it around with us.

You see, we can't find our self-worth based on what other people think of us. We must find our self-worth based on Christ and our relationship with Him. However, it doesn't seem to be that easy, and as life goes on, and we get a little older, we just tend to collect more baggage and carry it around with us.

Sometimes we pick up baggage from people who are close to us, like a best friend.

I wasn't the trendiest of my friends when I was younger. I had a best friend of mine that let me know how "untrendy" I was at a young age. The '80s were amazing times, and your slouch socks had to be just right with your Guess Jeans that had zippers up the side ankle.

One day, I showed up to play with my 'best friend,' and she informed me we couldn't play anymore because I didn't know how to dress right and wasn't cool enough. We were 'best friends forever,' and just like that forever, just got a lot shorter.

Your friends are trying to live life, just like you are, and they may make some poor decisions. You will get hurt by some of them, but if you don't learn to forgive, then you'll pick up some more baggage and carry it around as though it is a part of you.

You know, the truth about baggage is that we don't need other people to load it on us. We do a pretty good job of dumping baggage on ourselves when we compare ourselves to others. We think things like, "I'll never be as popular as they are," "I'll never be as talented as they are," "Why can't I be as good as they are?" When we listen to those thoughts in our heads, we pick up more baggage. We find ourselves saying, "They have it made," "Why is life so easy for them and so hard for me?" As we buy into that lie, we pick up more baggage.

Baggage can come from people we thought loved us, but they just don't realize that their words can cut like a knife. Maybe you were married, and your spouse had an affair; you were or are in an abusive relationship, your parents always told you that you wouldn't amount to anything, you're an accident, you weren't wanted anyways.

Most people don't mean to hurt us. It is just that they've got their baggage, and when you don't deal with baggage, you pass it on. If we find our identity in anything else other than our relationship with Christ, we pick up more baggage. When we hold on, we just collect even more, and it starts to get uncomfortable. Life is hard to manage and becomes tedious.

Our natural tendency is to want to dump this baggage on to someone else, but it always backfires. Your bad morning results in a short temper with your kids, a useless argument with your spouse, no patience with the bagger at the store that just put your eggs under your milk, or the old lady that cut you off and turned left in front of you before blaring your horn and telling her she is #1 with a finger gesture. Amid dumping some baggage off on someone else, you only end up picking up more for yourself.

Then there is that "other" suitcase. It's a sin, the secret sin. But it's cool because nobody knows about it. If I think I have it under control, then I have just picked up more baggage, and it has control of me. Even though no one else knows about it, God knows. We live our lives, and when we've got it all balanced out, maybe no one can really tell. You have learned to carry your baggage and balance it with your everyday life. But sometimes it gets unbalanced, and we find ourselves struggling just to stay up.

That's when you remember the words of Jesus, "I have come that you may have life and that you may have it abundantly." Let's be honest: Carrying baggage isn't an abundant life. You can't walk straight. The words of Jesus come to your mind again, "Come to me all you who are tired and worn out, and I will give you rest."

In those moments, we realize that is what we want. All we need to do is set our bags down before Jesus. He takes it; He takes it all, every single piece that we have collected. He says, "Come follow me. Leave it all behind. You didn't make the cut, but I have chosen you, and you are qualified because I am your Rabbi."

Jesus is going to make you just like Him. You're going to talk like Him, walk like Him, and you're going to do the things that He does. You just need to lay it all aside and walk away from it. Forget it. Oh, and by the way, He is going to make you a Rabbi. He is making you a teacher. He needs you to go to those around you and make disciples. Take those that are unqualified and qualify them by telling them about Jesus. Tell them and show them. Show them how He has changed you. Show them how you were unqualified but now are qualified!

Make disciples! Lay hands on the sick, set the captives free, bring deliverance to those in bondage, mend the brokenhearted, bring joy to those that mourn. You are now qualified. Even when you don't feel like it, remember that you are because He is your Rabbi, and you are becoming like Him!

Take courage. Jesus says to us, *"I no longer call you servants because a servant does not know his master's business. Instead, I have called you friends, for everything that I have learned from my Father I have made known to you."* (John 15:15)

COVER ME IN TIMES OF WAR

Joshua 11:13,
"But as for the cities that stood on their mounds, Israel burned none of them, except Hazor only, which Joshua burned."

COVER ME IN TIMES OF WAR

4. BURNOUT

Psalm 18:1-2 says,

> *"I will love You, O Lord, my strength. The Lord is my rock and my fortress and my deliverer; my God, my strength, in whom I will trust; My shield and the horn of my salvation, my stronghold."*

I love Psalm. David, along with Moses, is one of my favorite people. I have known this verse for a long time, but it wasn't until recently that I questioned what exactly the "horn of salvation" means. I tend to recite verses without really thinking about them. It makes me sound good, but really if I don't understand them, then what good does it do?

As I studied, I found out that a horn is a meaning for a lot of things. It is used metaphorically to signify strength and honor because horns are the weapons and ornaments of the animals that possess them. They are also used as a type of victory, emblems of power, dominion, glory, and fierceness, and they are also a chief means of attack and defense. On the flip side, the horn also can mean the peak or summit of a hill or the highest point.

Luke 1:68-69 says,

> *"Blessed is the Lord God of Israel, for He has visited and redeemed His people, and has raised up a horn of salvation for us in the house of His servant David,"*

So, a "horn of salvation" means the high point of salvation, the power, dominion, glory, and fierceness associated with our salvation. Jesus is the horn of salvation in our circumstances. He is the power and dominion, the glory, and fierceness; He is what we raise to be the highest point in our lives! HE IS OUR HOPE!

Isaiah 40:29-31 (Message Version) states,

> *"Why would you ever complain, O Jacob, or whine, Israel, saying, 'God has lost track of me. He doesn't care what happens to me?" Don't you know anything? Haven't you been listening? God doesn't come and go. God lasts. He's the creator of all you can see or imagine. He doesn't get tired out, doesn't pause to catch His breath. And He knows everything, inside and out. He energizes those who get tired, gives fresh strength to dropouts. For even young people tire and drop out, young folk in their prime stumble and fall. But those who wait upon God get fresh strength. They spread their wings and soar like eagles. They run and don't get tired; they walk and don't lag behind."*

Like these verses say, "He doesn't get tired out, doesn't pause to catch His breath. He gives strength to those who wait on the Lord." Whatever you have or are facing, whatever lies before you, God is already there.

Following one of my two favorite people, David and Moses, comes Joshua. He takes place on the scene in the Bible when Moses has died. He is now in charge. The people of God can now move into the Promised Land, but not without first overcoming those that stand in the way of their promise. This is what the people of God have left Egypt for; this is what they were afraid of forty years ago and had to wait until the old generation has passed. This is what God has promised to them, and now this is their moment, this is their hour, this is their time to seize what is before them!

Joshua is commissioned by God to now lead. He prepares the military, he sends spies into Canaan, makes a miraculous crossing of the Jordan river as it parts for Israel to cross, spared Rahab's life as they conquer Jericho, lost at Ai when they lost focus on God, went back and defeated Ai, has a significant failure when he makes a covenant with the wrong people, wins against the Amorites. Now we find ourselves in Joshua chapter 11. *(How's that for a tour of the Bible in the Susanne Ryan version?).* Joshua is on a roll. He has a few minor setbacks, but ultimately, he is seeing God move on his behalf.

Have you ever felt like life is going okay, you know God is there, you have had battles, but you know He is with you? Circumstances have come, but you have made it through. THEN – there is a breaking point. That moment when you realize things just got tough, life is hard. You know God is still there, but you feel you are like the reed who is bending and about to break. You have come to the tipping point where it can go either way. You are tired of being in battle, and everything is so hard. This is where Joshua is in chapter 11. That describes Israel's point in time.

Joshua 11:1-5,

> *"And it came to pass, when Jabin king of Hazor heard these things, that he sent to Jobab king of Madon, to the king of Shimron, the king of Achshap, and to the kings who were from the north, in the mountains, in the plains south of Chineroth, in the lowland, and in the heights of Dor on the west, to the Canaanites in the east and in the west, the Amorite, the Hittite, the Perizzite, the Jebusite in the mountains, and the Hivite below Hermon in the land of Mizpah. So, they went out, they and all their armies with them, as many people as the sand on the seashore in multitude, with very many horses and chariots. And when all these kings had met together, they came and camped together at the waters of Merom to fight against Israel."*

Well, that makes for a bad day. It is estimated that those against Israel came with over 20,000 horses and chariots. The Bible says, "As many people as the sand that is on the seashore." That makes all the conquest and the Jordan River parting dull in comparison to the opposition they now face.

Have you ever had a good day, week, month, or year, only to find yourself up against the most significant obstacle or battle you have ever faced? It is one day riding the victories and the next day hitting rock bottom. You can't see out of the fight you're in.

I counted sixteen different kings and kingdoms that came

against Joshua and the Israelites in Joshua 11. They banded together. Nothing like your enemies coming together as a front to take you on!

The king of Hazor, Jabin, was the one who rounded them all together. In the Susanne Ryan, expedited version of the story, Jabin told the other kings that "this Joshua guy is on his way with his God. He has been conquering those around us. Let's all band together and destroy Joshua and his army and his god! Let's show him who the real kings are!"

The good thing for Joshua is that his king is the actual King of all other kings! So, Joshua's King steps in and says this to him:

Joshua 11:6,

> *"But the Lord said to Joshua, "Do not be afraid because of them, for tomorrow about this time I will deliver all of them slain before Israel. You shall hamstring their horses and burn their chariots with fire."*

Hamstring the horses and burn the chariots!??? Why?

These kings had state of the art, the newest and the best chariots with the fastest horses known. Israel had come out of the desert. They had been there for forty years. They didn't have their hands on horses and chariots! I would imagine having grown up in a desert that when they crossed the Jordan River, they were thankful it parted. Not many places to learn to swim in the desert!

God told them to cut the hamstrings and burn the chariots because had they taken both things, they would have found their strength in the horses and chariots, not in God. They would have relied on the strength of the horses and the power of the chariots instead of the power and strength in the true King. God wanted to make sure that they stayed dependent on Him. He wanted to make sure they remembered who was fighting, and it wasn't the Israelites, but God.

Joshua 11:8-11,

> *"And the Lord delivered them into the hand of Israel, who defeated them and chased them... Until they left none of them remaining. So, Joshua did to them as the Lord had told him: he hamstrung their horses and burned their chariots with fire. Joshua turned back at that time and took Hazor, and struck its king with the sword; for Hazor was formerly the head of all those kingdoms. And they struck all the people who were in it with the edge of the sword, utterly destroying them. There was none left breathing. Then he burned Hazor with fire."*

Joshua 11:13,

> *"But as for the cities that stood on their mounds, Israel burned none of them, except Hazor only, which Joshua burned."*

Joshua knew that Hazor needed to be destroyed because Hazor was the stronghold and the one who gathered the kings and started the battles. Joshua knew he had to destroy Hazor himself. It was probably more symbolic to himself and those around him. It was Joshua saying, "No matter how strong you look in the physical, my God is stronger. No matter how big you are and how well known you are, my God is bigger than you'll ever dream of being."

You can't be intimidated by someone or something. Your circumstances won't make you fall or waiver. You'll be stable in all your ways because your ways are following God himself, the true King!

Joshua had burned the city of Hazor, and several times later, different kings had rebuilt it. In 1926, excavators dug up the town. As they dug down, layer after layer of civilization was shown until they got to the segment that had been around when Joshua made his appearance. The fire that Joshua had set was so intense that the stones along the wall, covered for hundreds of years, still had soot.

One man posted online that he visited the site and ran his hand along the wall with soot. He found himself realizing that it was like he stepped into the Bible itself. The fire that Joshua had set was so intense that it left a mark for hundreds of generations to be able to say, "Look what my God, our King, has done." It was evidence of the power of someone like Joshua, who was willing to submit his will and his life to the true King and God. God repays what the enemy steals. God redeems what the enemy has stolen. God is in our details.

Joshua was able to conquer and destroy the work of the enemy because he trusted God. He yielded all fear, all worry, a legitimate concern, and went forth in the mission that God had directed him to do. Only when Joshua became devoid of the elements that were not of God, could he be filled with the elements that were of God; God's mighty Spirit, going before him, raising him up as more than a conqueror.

We must take the option off the table of giving up. When we work with God, there is no giving up; there is just a giving until God. Give your will to God, your desires, your plans; He always makes it right.

I grew up a pastor's kids. I remember at around five years old that my dad sat me on the counter in our kitchen. He asked if I wanted to have Jesus in my heart. I was excited but didn't know why. How could God live in my heart? It didn't matter; I just prayed the prayer. I thought it was so exciting and knew that I asked if we could do it a few more times!

I was never the brightest kid in class. I always joke that I AM the no child left behind. I struggled in academics. I must work very hard to remember things and understand them; it has always been a struggle.

My sister and I both attended a Christian school growing up. During a special chapel one day at school, a missionary from Africa came. She told all about her work as a missionary. She showed pictures of them building homes, working with kids, giving out Bibles to those who have never heard of Jesus. I was so impressed, even as a six-year-old, that I wanted to be like her! I can remember many times someone would ask me what I wanted to be when I grew up, and I would always tell them that I wanted to be a missionary to Africa!

Then I reached fourth grade; I had a hard teacher. I'm sure

she was a good teacher, but she was tough. I still wasn't the brightest kid in class, but despite my academics and my insecurities, I knew who God was.

We were told one day to write an essay on what we wanted to be when we grew up. Of course, my essay was on being a missionary to Africa. I was proud of my essay. I told all about the big plans to be a missionary, just like the lady from the chapel.

Then the day came that we received our papers back with our grades. Mine was a big, fat, red "F." My teacher told me that my plans were unrealistic. I was supposed to write something I could do. I don't remember if I had to write the paper over or what happened except the only things that stuck in my fourth grade, academically challenged mind, was my teacher telling me that my dream of being a missionary was unrealistic. It stuck with me. If my teacher thought I couldn't do it then maybe I really couldn't!

One thing I undoubtedly inherited from my parents was my stubborn streak. I like to prove people wrong. So, when I was around fourteen years old, someone told me about a group called Teen Mania. Years later, it became known as Acquire the Fire. Teen Mania took youth on mission trips. This was my chance! I ordered the information packet, convinced my parents to let me go, and started raising money!

I left on Christmas day, flew across the country to Florida from California, where I met with a group of other teens. We were trained in drama and other areas, boarded a plane to a small island called

Eleuthera.

This island was impoverished. Most of them were farmers and fishermen. They lived in small shacks made of plywood and cardboard. We slept on the floor of a school and ate grits for most of our meals. It changed my life. I went home, realizing how much I had and didn't need and how much they needed and didn't have.

A few months later, I heard a lady at our church, Joanna Petronela. She mentioned she was going to Ukraine in a few months to take medicines to children affected by Chernobyl. I found her after service and asked if she ever takes anyone. I was only fourteen at the time, but she reluctantly said she takes groups of people with her when she goes. So, I, of course, asked if she would take me. I figured it was a 50/50 chance. She looked confused and said if I could raise the money, around $6,000 in a couple of months, then she would take me.

Challenge excepted. I called her back a few weeks later, told her I had the money, and what was my next step? She was even more confused but agreed to let me go.

I packed my clothes and stuff I needed, but the other half of my suitcase was bubble gum and stickers; hundreds of pieces of bubble gum and hundreds of stickers. I found a group in Los Angeles that would donate supplies, so I contact them, and they sent me over $2,000 worth of medical supplies and equipment to take with me.

My mom dropped me off at LAX International Flights, and off I flew to Russia and Ukraine for a few weeks!

We visited hospitals with kids who had cancer; we preached the Gospel on the streets, visited underground churches, prayed for the sick. It was, again, life-changing. I left Ukraine and Russia, and my life would never be the same. On my first mission trip, I saw the stuff they didn't have. This time I saw how they didn't know Jesus. It was hard for them to have a church, talk about God, just have a Bible, or someone to pray with them.

Not long after, I encountered a group called Adam's Children Fund. They ministered to orphans in Russia. I planned a trip again, and this time during my school break. I was now sixteen years old, a sophomore in high school.

I stayed with a small family. The mother was a doctor, Olga. She made around $20 a month in American money. She must've thought we were rich. And in her eyes, in her country, we were.

One orphanage that we visited, I learned that when kids turned sixteen, they were no longer able to live there. They had to find a job and a place to live in. As a sixteen-year-old myself, this hit home. This made many of them homeless and beggars. At another orphanage, we met many young children who had been there since birth. They didn't know what it was like to have a parent or a sibling. They slept in a large open room with many beds, used a large open bathroom, and ate in a small room. Many were brought very sick, and there were not enough workers so they would keep the sick children in a tiny crib, some only getting human contact a few times a day. One little girl lay in her bed, not very old and hadn't been there long. When we asked a worker what her name was, they just shrugged; she didn't have a name yet.

As we were on a bus going through town, we came across Russian soldiers on the side of the road. We had brand new Russian Bible's, so we stopped and passed them out. Some had never owned or seen a Bible. Being able to talk about Jesus was taboo in a communist country, but they had recently changed, and giving Bibles out was no longer against the law.

My life changed again.

Once back at home, I stood up on a Sunday morning to show the congregation pictures we had taken and to tell all that God did; many people had given financially. As I looked out, telling the story of what God did and what we saw, there was my fourth-grade teacher, sitting in the congregation. She probably didn't remember my essay and that she told me it was unrealistic, but I remembered.

It wasn't about what I did; it was about what God did. It was about what God can do and will do when you are willing to give over your life and your decisions to His ways and plans.

Our God is a redeeming God. He is the horn of our salvation. Whatever you have faced or are facing, He is greater! Whatever someone has said to you or about you, He is greater!

God doesn't take lightly the things that concern you. He won't leave you, and even if you feel like He has, know that He is right there with you in every detail of every day.

You may not be the smartest, strongest, the most good looking. You may not have a lot of money, things, or opportunities. People may look down on you, say things that aren't true, and bully you, but in the end, what matters is who you serve. As a servant of God, I know that my Master and King will supply all He has required of me!

Romans 12:3 says,
"For I say, through the grace given to me, to everyone who is among you, not to think of himself more highly than he ought to think, but to think soberly, as God has dealt to each one a measure of faith."

COVER ME IN TIMES OF WAR

5. LIVING BY FAITH

Did you know that your faith feeds on the Word of God? If you feed your faith, your doubts start to leave. Sounds simple, huh? Faith is what our relationship with God is based on. We have trust in that which we have faith in, and when we have a relationship with Jesus Christ, through faith, we, in turn, will trust Him.

Hebrews 11:1 and verse 6 says,

> *"(1) Now, faith is the substance of things hoped for, the evidence of things not seen. (6) But without faith, it is impossible to please Him, for he who comes to God must believe that He is and that He is a rewarder of those who diligently seek Him."*

Mark 11:22-24 says,

> *"So, Jesus answered and said to them, "Have faith in God. For assuredly, I say to you, whoever says to this mountain, 'Be removed and be cast into the sea,' and does not doubt in his heart, but believes that those things he says will come to pass, he will have whatever he says. Therefore,*

I say to you, whatever things you ask when you pray, believe that you receive them, and you will have them."

Have faith in God! Faith works for anybody, anytime, anyplace, anywhere. Faith works. Mark 11:23 said, *"Whosoever shall say to this mountain..."* Whosoever believes! Whosoever – it works for everybody! It will work for you if you're young, old, male, female, red, yellow, black and white, Mexican, African, European; faith works. Your faith will work for you.

Faith is a great equalizer. The world we live in is not a world of equality. The playing field is not always level. There is always someone out to cut you out and steal; the systems of the world are not designed for you to succeed. Most of the world is designed to keep you in mediocrity. You are easier to deal with when you're just average.

We live in a world that isn't always designed to help you succeed but is designed to keep you average, in debt, on medication, keep you in a box, and in a realm that you are manageable. However, God has given us something that will take us out of the box the world tries to put us in. God has told us to believe, and if we can believe, then all things are possible. If you're a new believer or if you've been in church for forty years, you can always learn something in your faith.

Faith is the message of empowerment that says, "I can believe my way out of what I'm in." We may not be able to control what zip code we grew up in, or who helped us or hurt us in the past, but we can be in charge of what we believe. If we can get faith down on the inside of us, no one can stop us from being what God has told us we could be.

No devil in Hell is a match for a believer that will put their feet down and say, "I'm going to believe my way over my situation." Christians are referred to as "Believers." Believers! *Stop and think about that one!* I am not intimidated by the world that says we use faith as a crutch. If you think my faith is a crutch, then you can just watch me limp my way out of here and into a blessing!

Just because you can't see faith doesn't mean it isn't real. Faith is a something. Faith is the 'substance of things hoped for'; you can't see it, but it is substance. Faith is more real than the chair you are sitting on, the book you are reading, or the car in your garage.

"As a man thinks in his heart, so is he." (Proverbs 23:7) It doesn't matter what people say to you; it matters what you say to yourself. If you think it in your heart, it doesn't matter what they call you. If you believe in your heart that you are a victor, then it doesn't matter that the world points and calls you crazy for believing in your faith.

People can call me a slow learner, the wrong side of the tracks and even dysfunctional, but when I say to myself "You can do all things through Christ," "You are more than a conqueror through Him that loves you," "You are able to go up and possess the land," all of their words fall to the ground because I have faith to believe in what He says about me. Faith puts me in a different position of those whose lives are ruled by rational. I am not an irrational person, illogical person; I just have something a little bit better and greater.

I can logic my way and reason my way through a situation, but I know that faith trumps reason and logic. Faith is higher than logic. There are things that my mind can't understand and that my faith must work around. God can say, "I am going to give you a destination," and my mind has no idea of how I will get there, but somewhere in my heart, I know that I walk by faith and not by sight.

Faith is not emotion. We don't believe in emotional for emotional sake. Emotionalism is defined as *having feelings that are easily excited and openly displayed.* I know people who live their lives based on emotionalism; every church service their emotions take over or every concert they faint. I believe we use our emotions like joy and enthusiasm, but faith should not be mistaken for emotion. If we live in emotionalism and our faith in Christ is based on such, then when the emotion is over, so is our faith.

Faith is not optimism. I'm a somewhat optimistic person, but faith is not optimism. Faith should not be mistaken for a good and positive attitude. Sometimes you wake up and have a positive attitude. "I feel like today is going to be a good day." It doesn't take but about three people to ruin that or two small humans getting ready for school. It is good to have the right attitude and to be optimistic, but my faith does not belong to the fluctuation of my mood. My emotions move my mood, and I don't know about you, but my emotions are the most unstable part of me.

Our emotions are like the wind; they go up and down based on what is happening around you. Faith is a spiritual force that resides on the inside of you, that is not moved by what you see, not driven by what you feel, by what somebody else has said to you; it is not run by how your migraine is today, whether your back is aching or what the balance your bank account shows. Faith is something that is moved only by the Word of God, and if God said it, then I'm going to stand on it. He said that if I believe, then anything is possible in my life!

You must give a voice to your faith, learn how to talk your faith, how to walk your faith, and work your faith. Faith is like a muscle; we must work it out. Some people spend their lives working on their muscles. You can have someone who spends a lifetime developing something and learning how to use it, grow it, feed it, and perfect it; other people just use it now and then.

In 2002, my husband Steve and I ran in the L.A. Marathon. He ran, and I somehow crossed the finish line a little over eight hours later. It was "somehow" because I'm not exactly sure how. All I know is that I passed the guy with no legs. No joke.

When I met my husband, he had already run several marathons, including half-marathons. A full marathon is 26.2 miles; that .2 of the 26 is a very LONG distance!

I decided it would be cool to run the marathon with my husband. How hard could this be? Thousands of people participate all the time! So, we signed up, and that March, we made our way to

L.A. with thousands of other "runners." I was excited. Steve is very much into working out, and I would work out now and then. Going to the gym is not on my top 1,000 things to do. I decided I would exercise a little more than usual, which wasn't much since I didn't exercise much in the first place. I also decided that I needed a new pair of shoes for this great event so I bought a nice new pair the week before the marathon.

If you have never participated in a marathon like the L.A. Marathon, let me tell you, it is intense. We started with around 20,000 people. Because I was inexperienced, I was placed far back in the group of thousands; the better and more experienced runners were closer to the front. It took a good twenty minutes to even get to the start line once the race started because there were so many people, crammed inches apart.

Once the start gunshot off I didn't have a choice to run because the thousands crammed so close inside my space bubble propelled me forward at a pace, I was not prepared to move. Nonetheless, the adrenaline kicked in, and I was running like Forrest Gump on a good day without braces.

Steve ran beside me, and by the time we reached the start line, approximately a mile from our original start place, I told him to go ahead, and I would meet him at the end. We decided to meet at the hotel when we finished the race and would wait for one another in the lobby.

This is probably a good place to stop and say that I have a lot of pride, quite a bit. So much that I needed to finish this race and not just start it because I had people at home who were very vocal about how there was no way I would be able to finish. Yes. I am prideful, and I admit it. Enough said.

So, as I ran, Steve ran ahead of me. Every mile, there was a mile marker sign that would display what mile you were at in the race as well as how much time had passed since the start of the race. They also had tables set up with tiny little cups of juice or pieces of banana and oranges. The best part was I was so excited to be one of the runners to eat an orange slice or drink a small cup of water and toss it to the ground. That's what you do when you run a race; it's cool. You are part of the club when you get to do those running things. Plus, there was a huge crowd that was along the closed Los Angeles roads that cheered me on. The big number on the front of my shirt also had my first name, SUSANNE. It was big enough for people to read and yell, and it propelled me further when I would hear it.

Around mile 6, I realized I was losing my adrenaline; this was getting hard now. Granted, I had 20.2 more miles to run, but my very white chick body was quickly being fried in the sun. I'm like a magnet for sun rays; I'm so white that I'm like a mirror reflecting the beams in all directions. I fry like a lobster, and although I was only around mile 6, I could feel my sunscreen slowly failing me.

At one point, two ladies slowly jogged past me, armed with their fanny packs full of surprises. As they jogged near me, I saw them rub on sunscreen to their faces and shoulders. I jogged in their direction, and politely asked if they could spare a little, to which they giggled and promptly said, "Sorry, we only have enough for ourselves." They upped their jogging pace and sped off like high school teens in a club of their own.

I think it was around mile 11 that I realized there was this strange pain coming from my feet. My jog had turned into a slightly fast-paced walk as I rounded a corner to a First-Aid station. I grabbed an orange slice and sat down in the medic's chair. After explaining the pain in my feet, I took off my brand-new shoes and socks and revealed a few quarter size blisters on both feet; some on the back of my heels, some on the ball of my feet and a few on my toes. The medic asked if I had worn my shoes much before the race, to which I explained in a proud voice that they were brand new! It was then that I realized you're not supposed to wear brand new shoes to a marathon; it's best to break them in first. *(Keep that information in your brain storage somewhere in case you ever decide to run a marathon! -- You're welcome --)*. The medic sprayed lidocaine on my feet, a little ointment and bandages, and off I was to jog some more. Lucky me.

After my first bandage experience, I found that I was now stopping at almost every First-Aid station for more lidocaine. The pain reliever wasn't working very long, and the constant rubbing of my brand-new shoes on blisters eventually opened the blisters into sores and more blisters.

The rest of my body could have used an overhaul at that point as well since I was effectively now bright red from the sun, and every joint on my body was aching. I was like the video clips of marathon runners you see that hobble the last quarter mile to the finish; the difference is that I wasn't even halfway through! I knew by the clock at the mile markers that Steve was probably finished with the race by now. I'm sure he would be wondering where I was, but he would have to sit and wonder for much longer because this was going to take a while.

By mile 23, the First-Aid medic highly recommended that I take the bus back to the start, but I didn't want to quit, I couldn't quit. I had too much pride. I had to finish. He told me all the other water stations were now closed and no more First-Aid stations either. I would have to go the last few miles with him taking me back or go on my own. I knew if I stepped on the bus, I was out of the race. Although, at this point, I'm not sure who I was racing against since most of the 20,000 had probably finished.

I let him spray my feet with lidocaine again, bandage them, and set back out to finish. Roads, at this point, were now open back up to traffic, so I found myself at the crosswalks waiting for the light to change. I was surrounded by about 30 other marathoners – mostly all in their 80's.

I came around the corner to the last mile where we had to cross over a bridge. There were no longer crowds to cheer me on, just one woman on a sidewalk. As I hobbled down the street, and hobble is being gracious, I heard her yell, "You can do it, Susan!" This would usually motivate me, but through my now sobbing tears, I said, "My name is not Susan, it's SUSANNE!!"

I contemplated sitting down on the sidewalk, but my hips and knees, shoulders, elbows, finger knuckles, heck, every bone and nerve in my body ached. I knew I wouldn't be able to stand up again if I sat, so I lifted each leg with my hands and kept moving while sobbing.

Had I trained and been disciplined, I could have made that marathon a lot easier on myself. Other people made it look so easy, but they made it look easy because they trained for it. Faith is this way. It is like a muscle, and you must use it.

There is a thing called common faith. It means that God has dealt unto every man a measure of faith.

Romans 12:3 says,

> *"For I say, through the grace given to me, to everyone who is among you, not to think of himself more highly than he ought to think, but to think soberly, as God has dealt to each one a measure of faith."*

Faith is a seed. That means that you have the same faith seed form that the Apostle Paul had, or Abraham, or Moses! Your spirit is the same as anybody you want to read about in the Bible, anyone in history, you have the same faith in a seed form. You need to learn how to water it and start working it.

You don't know where to start? Well, you don't have to start big; you just start somewhere. It says it is a seed, and Jesus said faith is like a grain of mustard seed – so tiny but can grow into something substantial and unrecognizable. He isn't talking about size, but about potential. Your faith is small, but the potential is great! God will give you a context to practice your faith. You must practice it somewhere and learn how to exercise your faith in greater things.

When I was a teenager, I was challenged in my giving and my faith. I was given a beautiful antique ring. It was a large brown topaz stone in the middle with diamonds and antique gold all around. I loved it. Then a year later, a special speaker came to our church and talked about giving and faith. They preached about how sometimes we hold onto our stuff and our money because we put our faith in our stuff. They challenged people to give as they never have before.

This was in the first service on a Sunday morning. I took my ring, and between services, I went to my dad's office, who is the pastor, and handed the speaker my ring. I said, "this is the most expensive thing I own, but I want to give it away." I believed by faith that God could match and go above whatever I was believing for.

About two weeks later, someone at our church came and handed me a small box. Inside was a diamond cluster ring; it was beautiful, fit perfect, and probably worth even more than the last ring. I kept it and wore it, knowing God gave it in response to my faith last time. Now my faith was moving and growing. I thought for sure I was on to something!

A year later, I had a good friend who was getting married. She and her fiancé didn't have a lot of money, and I wanted to help them out, so I gave my new diamond ring to her to use as a wedding ring. In all honesty, in the back of my mind, I thought, "Ha! If God gave me this nicer ring last time, I wonder what He will give me this time!" ...and away, my ring went...

It would make for a great story to say that two weeks later, I received another ring worth double than the last, but that didn't happen. I waited, but it didn't happen. Faith is not a formula; faith is a relationship.

I had to learn a hard lesson: It isn't what God gives me, but it is what He gives me that He makes act like something else. He takes my $20 and makes it act like $200; it goes further. He takes the widow's flour and makes it last longer. He takes the oil and makes it fill every container.

Faith has a way of moving on the inside of you, giving you a context when you're in a position of smallness or feel boxed in, or you can't see your way out, it isn't matching up to where you thought you would be at a time in life. Those are the moments to look around and see that God is giving me a context by which to exercise my faith that will reveal itself later down the road. It is the same as sowing seed and working on your muscles; it just gets bigger as you learn to work them.

Mark 10:46-52 says,

> *"Then they came to Jericho. And as He went out of Jericho with His disciples and a great multitude, blind Bartimaeus, the son of Timaeus,*

sat by the road begging. And when he heard that it was Jesus of Nazareth, he began to cry out and say, 'Jesus, Son of David, have mercy on me!' Then many warned him to be quiet, but he cried out all the more, 'Son of David, have mercy on me!' So, Jesus stood still and commanded him to be called. Then they called the blind man, saying to him, 'Be of good cheer. Rise, He is calling you.' And throwing aside his garment, he rose and came to Jesus. And Jesus answered and said to him, 'What do you want me to do for you?' the blind man said to Him, 'Rabboni, that I may receive my sight.' Then Jesus said to him, 'Go your way; your faith has made you well.' And immediately, he received his sight and followed Jesus on the road."

I certainly don't want to imply that Jesus didn't want to heal Bartimaeus, but He didn't initiate this miracle, blind Bartimaeus did. Verse 47 says, *"And when he heard that it was Jesus of Nazareth. . ."* He hears something; he can't see, but he can certainly hear something. But wouldn't Bartimaeus have listened to a lot of things? There he was in the middle of a crowd, a quite large one, so it most certainly had to be loud.

Romans 10:17 says, *"So, then faith comes by hearing, and hearing by the Word of God."*

John 1:1 says, *"In the beginning was the Word, and the Word was with God, and the Word was God."*

Something happens when you hear the Word, and Bartimaeus listened to the Word Himself, he heard Jesus, God, speak.

The dominant sound in their life determines people's lives. If you surround yourself with negativity, it will defeat your faith; the sound of gossip and unbelief in your life will taint your growth. You must get the right sound over your life.

When Bartimaeus heard Jesus was coming by, he began to cry out. He may not have his sight, but he can hear and can shout! He began to call for Jesus to have mercy. You need enough faith to lose your pride, with your whole world falling apart, throw up your hand, and say, "Jesus have mercy on me!"

It says that many charged him to hold his peace. Anytime you begin to walk by faith, you are moving upstream. You can't expect everybody around you to understand what your faith means; you can't expect everyone to get into agreement with you. Most of the people around us in our lives are so content and comfortable, they're doing the same old thing, and their entire lives rotate around working all week long to be able to buy a couple of lottery tickets. They want to do the same old same old because it is too much work to go upstream.

Faith has a voice; it is not emotional. When they told Bartimaeus to be quiet, he simply got louder because he realized he must be getting closer to his goal! Somewhere in life, you need to have a little push back in your faith. When the world tells you, "No, don't go," you must push back harder. When your mind tells you that you're not going to make it, you need to find some faith on the inside of you and make the voice of praise bigger than the voice of doubt. You need to make the voice of Jesus louder over your head than the voice that is trying to come against you. When you're moving forward in faith, you don't have time to be passive; you can't afford to sit there.

Blind Bartimaeus knew his only answer was Jesus. We need to have as much tenacity as he had, realizing that our only solution is in Jesus. Your only answer is Jesus! You're smart, but not that smart; you're strong, but not that strong; you have a lot going for you, but you don't have it all. You better put your trust in Jesus! That's why God gave you faith on the inside of you so that you can bridge the gap between where you are and where He is. He gave you the gift of faith so you can realize that when you are limited, He is not limited, and when you can't see a way, He can make a way!

When you know Jesus is passing by, get your faith out, and call him! The Scripture says that "Jesus stood still." The same Jesus that was about to pass by him stopped when He found out Bartimaeus's faith would not be detoured. In the face of opposition, rather than shrinking away, he became stronger. The miracles in life that are passing you by will stop if you dare to open your mouth and call His name. If you will quit throwing a pity party and quit crying for yourself if you will shake yourself and stir up your faith, then you will find out a miracle is on its way to your house!

Believe your way out of what you are in. If you could see me in my future and where I'm going, without my beggars' garment, no depression, without this trouble, you would thank God for me, and you would see me not where I am at but where I'm going! Live by faith!

Exodus 3:2-3 says,
"And the Angel of the Lord appeared to him in a flame of fire from the midst of a bush. So, he looked, and behold, the bush burned with fire, but the bush was not consumed. Then Moses said, "I will now turn aside and see this great sight, why the bush does not burn.""

COVER ME IN TIMES OF WAR

6. BIGGER PICTURE

I love to read, and I especially love to read fiction stories that are written around biblical events. One of my favorite people in the Bible is Moses. He is someone that I will be visiting regularly in Heaven. I want to know all the details of his random anger issues, his experience of the parting of the Red Sea, the days on the mountain with God, and growing up a Prince of Egypt.

When we read the story of Moses, we find that the people of Israel are living as slaves in Egypt. They didn't start there in bondage and slavery. The people of God were brought to Egypt by Joseph and Pharaoh when Joseph saw his brothers after they had sold him into slavery. But now Israel found themselves in a situation where all they know is bondage and slavery. This is their life.

Moses is born in a time when Pharaoh is murdering all baby Hebrew boys. He is born into slavery and given away by his parents to save his life. The daughter of Pharaoh finds him. He grows up as an Egyptian in the palace with everything he could ever want or desire.

It sounds like an exciting start to a good movie!

Then one day, Moses murders an Egyptian who he finds beating a Hebrew slave. Now once again, he is an outcast. He is set apart from his family at birth only to be set apart from his royal family as well. His only choice is to leave Egypt. He leaves all he has ever known, both good and bad, and starts on a new life. He marries, has children, and even a new career.

We then reach Exodus 3, and here stands Moses, the man who was once a slave, part of a royal family, and is found now as a simple shepherd in the wilderness. That's a far cry from a palace or a mud pit for bricks. This is a man with a lengthy testimony of his life of tragedy. He has had a full life of trials and obstacles. And then God . . . But God. I like big Buts!

Exodus 3:2-3 says,

"And the Angel of the Lord appeared to him in a flame of fire from the midst of a bush. So, he looked, and behold, the bush burned with fire, but the bush was not consumed. Then Moses said, "I will now turn aside and see this great sight, why the bush does not burn."

"I will turn aside and see this great sight" means to stop the direction you are going and go somewhere else. I don't know about you, but if a tree is on fire for no apparent reason, I am pretty sure I am going to stop what I'm doing and check it out.

Exodus 3:4,

> *"So, when the Lord saw that he turned aside to look, God called to him from the midst of the bush and said, "Moses, Moses!" And he said, "Here I am!"*

God called out to him from the midst of the bush. The word called is the same word that was used in Genesis when God "called" the light day and the darkness night and when God "called" the heavens and separated the dry land and the seas. Not only did Moses stop to see what was happening, but then the happening started to talk! It called him out!

God showed up and in a burning bush no less! Moses did the right thing, and he turned aside to look. In the middle of his circumstances, his life that has not been so smooth and easy, he turns to look in God's way. Amid the burning bush, in the middle of a random day, Moses sees God and hears God in His circumstance.

I don't know about you, but I would've questioned the herbal tea I drank that morning, or I would've wondered if I had been around the sheep too long. Yet, Moses stopped to listen to a burning bush that was talking. It wasn't a cartoon voice like the Moses movies or a comical voice like Mickey Mouse, but I imagine it to be a voice so distinct that Moses heard it in every part of himself.

We all have a story. Some of us have had an excellent start to life, and some haven't. Some have had a loving family growing up, and some not so much. But here you are, in your circumstance, whatever that may look like. Let me be the voice in the burning bush for you today! God wants you to look aside from the mundane of your life, from the day to day, from the not so good, 'why did it happen?', 'where was God?' moments – and look in His direction. Listen to His voice. There is a bigger picture, a more excellent plan. It is how you respond; it is your reaction and action that is going to matter the most.

A couple of years ago, my husband and I were rudely awakened around one o'clock in the morning. My husband, Steve, woke me up to tell me he thought he had heard one of our girls crying. We crept out of bed to find them sound asleep, but we both heard a faint noise. We quietly shut their doors and followed the noise. As we walked out to our living room, we realized something was off.

Our home is on a corner of the cul-de-sac, and our living room has windows in the corner that face the street. Instead of our home being dark for the night, it was now lit up with light all around and a distant noise in the background that yelled a muffled voice that was saying, "come out with your hands up."

We both looked at each other with perplexed looks and asked, "Are they saying our address and calling our names?" It couldn't be. This was strange and didn't make any sense, a bizarre dream for sure. After a few more moments, we listened more and peered out our window to see what was happening, but all we could see was floodlights shining straight into our home, and a strange voice calling what we were thinking was our name and address.

I picked up my phone and dialed 9-1-1.

"9-1-1, what is your emergency?"

"Yes," I said, "I'm trying to find out if you are outside of our home right now?" I then gave the nice lady at the end of the phone our address.

"Yes, ma'am. The police are outside. Is there a Steve Ryan with you?"

"Yes, my husband is right here."

"Okay, he needs to go outside right now with his hands up."

"He what?" I said in a panicked voice.

"He needs to go out now. Send him out now to the police. They are outside."

So, of course, I turned to Steve and said, "You need to go out!"

My poor husband. I didn't delay in sending him to whatever was happening outside.

"You have to go out!" I said again.

He calmly walked into the restroom.

That's when the nice 9-1-1 lady said, "Is he coming out? I need to let the police know."

"Um, yeah. He is going to come out. He is in the restroom."

I quickly put our small dog in the backyard, and after just a few moments, Steve came out, and we opened the front door to the unknown bright lights. A blaring megaphone shouted for Steve to put his hands in the air and walk towards them. I watched for a few moments as they guided him down our driveway, walking backward now, and then I ran back in the house as the nice 9-1-1 lady said, "You need to get ready to go out when he reaches the police.

I picked up my cell phone and called my father, a Chaplain, and pastor. He didn't answer, so I quickly text him, "Dad! I don't know what is happening, but the police are here and just took Steve outside, and I'm next. The girls are still asleep. I don't know what is going on. Please call!"

I then, as only a woman would do, ran into our bedroom with the nice lady on the phone, put my socks on, got my glasses, and fixed my hair (it is crazy curly hair). I did all that just in time as the nice lady on 9-1-1 said, "Okay, you need to hang up the phone and go out with your hands up." I politely and awkwardly said, "Okay, thank you for your help," then hung up the phone and started through the same door my husband had recently disappeared.

The megaphone blared again, directing me to do the same that Steve had just done. I quickly put my hands in the air and walked backward down our driveway and towards the bright lights. As I reached the megaphone voice, they told me to turn around, at which I was now facing the end of a sizeable semi-automatic police-issued gun. The up side was that I could hear my husband chatting to another officer. I always say he has a way of even making a wall talk. It was no surprise he had probably made friends with the SWAT team already.

As I turned around and realized it was the SWAT team and local police, they then asked, "Ma'am, has your husband been keeping you and your daughters' hostage inside your home?"

"No," I said.

"Is there anyone else in your home besides your two girls?"

"No," I said again.

They then led me to my husband and told us that someone had called in an incident saying, "There is a Pastor Steve who lives on the corner, blue house. He has a black SUV car in the driveway and is holding his wife and two little girls' hostage in their garage. He is saying he will kill them if he doesn't get cocaine and $10K."

Huh. Nice. Yeah, that wasn't happening. We stood there shocked, still wondering what the heck was happening and how strange and bizarre all of this seemed. The police told us that they needed to walk through our home as a precaution. So, with their guns drawn, we gave them an excellent little tour of the inside of our humble abode.

As they reached our bedroom, located at the back of our house, the office stated that there was "obviously nothing that matched the story and all is clear," to which my husband, of course, said, "Well, we do need the $10,000 still." I laughed, cops did not.

In the days following, more of the story slowly came out. The lieutenant from the evening visited us the following day to let us know what had happened. A young, teenage boy from across the street had been playing games online and chatting in the online chat room. His "friends" dared him to "swat" someone, so he called the police to report an incident at a Walmart in Texas. After making that call, the SWAT team was sent to two locations on a false report. The teenage boy was then dared to "swat" a neighbor. Lucky for us, he knew enough information to make a semi-detailed call to the local police.

The lieutenant explained that they had figured out who the boy was because he had given a wrong address, which resulted in the SWAT team visiting the homes on our block to find a "Pastor Steve." Most of our neighbors pointed to our house, where the only "Pastor Steve" lived with a wife and two little girls. The police traced the call to the boy's home, arrested him, and took him that same day, only to release him because he was too young to charge and keep.

Steve and I decided to go and speak to the family. We walked across the street to his home and asked his parents if we could talk with them. Ten minutes later, we walked back home after having a conversation with the family, expressing to them and the boy that we would not hold a grudge and that we were there if they needed anything. The boy cried as he told us how sorry he was. It seemed like a change of heart and a God moment.

The next day, the young boy came over in tears. As I sat with him in our front yard, he said, "I just don't understand. Why would you guys forgive me so easily?" It didn't take me long to answer as I knew that this was most definitely a God moment.

I stated, "Because the God I serve has so easily forgiven us. We forgive you. We want you to know this same God." We spoke a few more moments, and I told him that Steve would come to talk to him when he returned home from work. Steve ended up driving the young boy to church with us that evening. It was awkward, but we did our best, and so did he, to find the good.

A few years have passed since the incident, and the boy has moved recently. However, in those few years, he found our home to be a place of refuge when things got bad. He made his way across the street to our front door several times, in tears, as he needed counseling and advice. Steve was always gracious, and before they moved to another state, the young boy's sister and fiancé were married by my husband.

There was a bigger picture. This incident could have gone so bad, so quickly, but it didn't. We had no idea what would unfold in the years after that night. It doesn't make Steve or myself any better than anyone else. It just makes the point that God can turn any situation for good when we allow Him into our story.

Going back to our original story: As you may know, Moses went on to lead millions of Israelites to freedom. We read the story often as though it was a couple of days or just a few years, but it was his life. It was a constant moving, changing, hearing, listening, following, doubting, struggling – but turning aside to do what God needed.

Moses made mistakes. You will make mistakes. I will continue to make mistakes. This is life, and yet God uses even each mistake to show Himself strong and make His name known!

We find a point in Moses's life that he stands at the outskirts of the people of God's promise: Canaan Land. God has promised them a new land, a land of milk and honey. He has promised something they have always wanted, yet never had. They have seen miracle after miracle. Each miracle God moves on their behalf over and over. They complain, and God moves. They are in need and murmur; God moves. They are sad, they rejoice. They sin, God forgives. It is up and down for a whole generation.

So now they are outside their promise. Caleb and Joshua have come back from being spies to their promised land, and they are saying, "We are able! We can do this! You can't tell me God sent ten plagues, opened the Red Sea, fed us with manna, water from a rock, fire in a cloud, the victory in the battle, and now we will be run out by giants!?"

Let me tell you!!! There is more to your story! Don't give up. Don't give in. It may look bad, but I am the voice in your desert. "Look towards God!" Just let God be God and be free from yesterday!

I am going to take God's promises. He is the same God as in

the Old and New Testaments. I'm not under; I'm over. I'm over these giants in my life. I don't have less than enough; I have more than enough. I'm not a victim, I've been called to be a victor!

Something happens along our journey in life. You can't go into tomorrow with a lack and limitation spirit, blaming everybody else. You must get the power of God in your life. You can do this. You have a promise to contend for; God spoke it, and it is true. God spoke it, and you're going to walk in it!

LET THE
FIRE FALL

Hebrews 12:29 says,
"For our God is a consuming fire."

7. LET THE FIRE FALL

Years ago, in Yosemite National Park, they had what was called the Fire Falls. The locals would gather old bark and dead trees and place them at the top of Glacier Point. The fire would burn for hours and become a mass pile of hot, red embers. Around 9'oclock in the evening, the people below in the camp would yell to the top of the mountain, "Let the fire fall!" Their cry would echo up to the top of Glacier Point, where the workers would begin to push the embers off the side of the cliff; it would create a beautiful, hot, red, fire fall that looked like a waterfall.

What an amazing event to encounter; it translates so well into our everyday walk with Christ. "Let the fire fall!" It is often an anthem in revival; we cry out for more of God in our churches, our communities, our personal lives, and even our governments.

Fire is a symbol of deity. The Bible talks of the fire as a symbol of the Holy Spirit. Hebrews 12:29 says, *"For our God is a consuming fire."*

Matthew 3:11 says, *"He will baptize you with the Holy Spirit and fire."* Fire is also a symbol of acceptance and approval by God. In the Old Testament, when they offered an offering to God, they knew that God approved of their offering because the fire would fall from heaven and consume the sacrifice.

Leviticus 9:22-24,

> *"Then Aaron lifted his hand toward the people, blessed them, and came down from offering the sin offering, the burnt offering, and peace offerings. And Moses and Aaron went into the tabernacle of meeting, and came out and blessed the people. Then the glory of the Lord appeared to all the people, and fire came out from before the Lord and consumed the burnt offering and the fat on the altar. When all the people saw it, they shouted and fell on their faces."*

Fire is also a symbol of God's presence. Wherever God was, there was a demonstration of fire. Zechariah 2:5, *"For I,' says the Lord, 'will be a wall of fire all around her, and I will be the glory in her midst."* God led the children of Israel by a pillar of fire by night. The fire had a guiding effect, illuminating their way to their freedom.

God is calling the church again to be a people consumed by the fire of God, a people consumed by the Holy Spirit who shows Himself strong in our lives. He is calling His church to be consumed by the fire of the Holy Spirit, who comes and accepts us and approves of who we are in Christ. Some of us, most of us, need that passion again. That passion that stands and yells, "Let the fire fall!" Let us be people who are ready to be consumed by the fire of God!

Romans 12:1,

> *"I beseech you therefore, brethren, by the mercies of God, that you present your bodies a living sacrifice, holy, acceptable to God, which is your reasonable service."*

Lord, let your fire fall! When programs replace passion and power, it is time for the fire. When worship becomes mechanical, it is time for the fire. When we are bathed in immorality, and we are no longer convicted, it is time for the fire!

2 Timothy 1:6,

> *"Therefore, I remind you to stir up the gift of God, which is in you through the laying on of hands."*

The Amplified Bible says it this way,

> *"That is why I would remind you to stir up (rekindle the embers of, fan the flame of, and keep burning) the [gracious] gift of God,"*

We must be willing to fuel the flames of God within us, knowing that it stirs the gift of God that He has placed in our lives.

Provers 26:20 says, *"For lack of wood, the fire goes out, and where there is no whisperer, contention ceases."* Fire comes from the Lord, but we must keep it burning in our lives! We must keep wood on the fire, and if you don't put wood on the fire, all you have is old ashes. What is wood on the fire? Bible reading is wood on the fire; prayer is wood on the fire, worship is wood on the fire, praise is wood on the fire, living holy and forgiving your enemies, resisting temptation when no one is looking... Keep the firebox full of wood! It is the everyday living right, making the hard choices, doing the Godly things – that is fueling the fire of God within you. Fan the flame. Let the fire fall!

Have you ever been burned by fire? It makes you move! When I burn my hand on the stove, it makes me jump! It makes me move and startles me! It is about time that some of us had some fire that made us move! When was the last time you had the fire of the Holy Spirit in your life make you jump and move? A touch of the fire will heal our families, burn out addictions and habits, give deliverance to people. Let the fire fall!

We need tongues of fire that the book of Acts talks about. The fire of the Holy Spirit came upon the 120 in the upper room, and by the time they moved outside, they couldn't help but tell people about Jesus. Peter even stood amid the crowd and yelled the well-known Scripture from Joel 2:28-32:

> *"And it shall come to pass afterward that I will pour out My Spirit on all flesh; Your sons and your daughters shall prophesy, your old men shall dream dreams, your young men shall see visions. And also, on My menservants and on My maidservants, I will pour out My Spirit in those days. And I will show wonders in the heavens and in the earth; blood and fire and pillars of smoke. The sun shall be turned into darkness, and the moon into blood, Before the coming of the great and awesome day of the Lord. And it shall come to pass that whoever calls on*

the name of the Lord shall be saved."

That's bold! There was a fire in him that he couldn't keep to himself! Over 3,000 people were saved that day. When the fire comes, it brings conviction. When was the last time you felt God's conviction? Not condemnation, but conviction! How many people push away the fire when they feel it rising inside of them? If we were willing, we would see that fire grow into a conviction that spreads like wildfire to all those around us. It is contagious; it is consuming; it spreads and moves quickly.

After the crucifixion of Jesus, there were two men on the road to Emmaus. The risen Christ walked with them, and they didn't even know it, but once they realized who He was they said: (Luke 24:32) *"And they said to one another, "Did not our heart burn within us while He talked with us on the road, and while He opened the Scriptures to us?"*

We are the temple of the Holy Spirit, God Himself resides by the Holy Spirit within us. When was the last time that your life or your words left someone saying, "Did not my heart burn within me? I knew something was different!" When was the last time you had a fire, a burning for the things of God?

I was in the grocery store not long ago, minding my own business, walking down the bread aisle. As I looked for my favorite brand of bread, a lady with an electric store cart pulled up beside me. Again, I was minding my own business. I just wanted to get in and out of the store, and it had already been a long day. She crept closer and closer to me. I saw her out of the corner of my eye and thought an old lady in an electric cart being a creeper seemed odd, so I asked if I could help her. Maybe she needed help getting something off the higher shelf?

Instead of helping her with a loaf of bread, I found myself being told a story by an old lady in an electric shopping cart. She started to tell me her story of a recent stroke. She had been living her life, and one day had a stroke, no sign that she recognized something was about to change her life, just a stroke that changed it all.

At first, I was annoyed. I wasn't interested in the ramblings of an old lady who just started talking to me in the bread aisle, but then I realized this was a God moment. I needed to pay attention. She must have recognized something in me that she would roll her electric store cart in my direction. Why me? What drew her to tell me, of all people, her story? Because I have the Holy Spirit. She wasn't drawn to me; she was drawn to that which resides within me! I listened intently, and when she took a breath (it was a long story), I asked if I could pray with her.

Have you ever noticed that most people will never turn down prayer? They usually mumble, "Yes, you can pray" and then quickly bow their heads and close their eyes. She smiled broadly and agreed, and we began to pray. She didn't jump out of her electric grocery cart; she didn't scream and yell. She simply said "Amen" and rolled off with a satisfied smile on her face.

In all honesty, I almost didn't pray for her. My flesh got in the way, I was preoccupied with my wants and needs, but that is nothing new for me. I deal with my flesh and selfish ways daily. It comes down to this: Either we believe the Bible, or we don't! If we believe it, then we need to act on it! How can we keep it quiet? How can we keep it from others?

Jeremiah was tired of being the one to tell people what God wanted. He wasn't a popular person because he said it like it was. He told the truth, but he got tired of being God's messenger and said this:

(Jeremiah 20:7-13)

> *"You pushed me into this, God, and I let you do it. You were too much for me. And now I'm a public joke. They all poke fun at me. Every time I open my mouth I'm shouting, "Murder!" or "Rape!" and all I get for my God-warnings are insults and contempt. But if I say, "Forget it! No more God-messages from me!" The words are fire in my belly, a burning in my bones. I'm worn out trying to hold it in. I can't do it any longer!"*

Let us be a people so full of the fire of the Holy Spirit that we cannot hold it back! We cannot stay silent or keep it to ourselves. There is a world, nations, and people who need to hear what God has said. We must fan the flame and rekindle the fire! Make people stop and ask, "What is different about you?" Tell them it is Jesus!

Stand at the foot of the mount, at the feet of Jesus, at the foot of the cross, and say, "Let the fire fall!" Yesterday's ashes won't do anymore. The people out there, our community, our nation, need the fire of God. They need the Holy Spirit, who speaks truth in love, who offers hope, who gives joy when they are mourning, gives beauty for ashes! We are a people of the fire of the Holy Spirit. We must stir up the gift and awaken our hearts.

Miracles, signs, and wonders are amazing, but no man can heal you or save you except Jesus. The greatest miracle is that of salvation! When the fire of God hits our lives, it burns up all that does not belong. Sickness and diseases can't stay in the fire. He was wounded for our transgressions, and by His stripes, we are healed physically, emotionally, and spiritually. He heals us from our addictions and bondages. By His stripes, we are healed!

David wrote in Psalm 69:9, *"The zeal for Your house has eaten me up!"* Let us be a people like Jeremiah that says, *"Your Word is like fire shut up in my bones, and I cannot contain it!"* Be the fire that someone else needs! Spread the fire within you, spark a passion in someone else with the power of God within you.

Let the fire fall!

Psalm 121:1-2,
"I look up to the mountains – does my help come from there?
My help comes from the Lord, who made heaven and earth!"

8. TELL YOUR MOUNTAIN

Psalm 121:1-2,

> *"I look up to the mountains – does my help come from there?*
> *My help comes from the Lord, who made heaven and earth!"*

It is believed that at the time that David wrote this Psalm, he was most likely on a pilgrimage to Jerusalem. Traveling back then was not like traveling now; it was not a quick trip to and from in the family van. Traveling was a full-on journey.

Israel was known as the people who worshipped the "unseen" God. All other religions worshipped something like an idol, an object, a person, an element of nature, but Israel worshipped the "unseen" God. This had to be quite confusing to other religions because gods were meant to be seen. When they worshipped their gods, they would place a temple or statue of their gods at their high points. Hilltops and mountains were marked by idol worship; that was their way of making their god known in their region. Traveling to an area, a visitor would have no problem identifying who the people worshipped since it was the high point for all to see.

Israel was different; they worshipped the unseen God. They were not permitted to make an idol to worship, an object of affection. How can you worship a God you believe made it all? God didn't even want them to have a king because He knew that a king would become like an idol, a point of affection, and worship to the people.

When David says in Psalm 121, "I look up to the mountains – does my help come from there?", he is saying in essence, "I look up to the mountains, on my journey, in what I am going through, does my help come from what I can see? No! My help comes from the Lord, the one who has made the heaven's and the earth!" He is saying that nothing the world has to offer or present to him can help him. Only the One who made it all can step in for what he needs.

Tell your mountain about your God! Just when I think my faith is strong, I am hit with a life circumstance that reminds me that my faith seems weak. When I have faith, I can have hope. I cannot have hope without faith. I hope in something because I have faith in that something. When hope seems lost or weak, it is because my faith is weak or being challenged.

Someone who does not believe in God does not lose hope in God because they never had faith in Him in the first place. I tend to make God small. He becomes like an idol in my life that I put on the hilltop. He isn't a genie to be at our call. He isn't a wish master who grants whatever we want or seem to need. He is God. I can make

God small enough in my mind and my faith that He becomes what I call a Pocket Jesus. I make Him my pocket idol. If I can view my God at my level, then I can understand Him. I can comprehend why things do or don't happen. He is on my level; I can see Him. But that is not the case.

We must remember that when we approach God, we are immediately at a deficit. It is hard for us to understand God because He is so God, and we are not. God is so God that if God had chosen not to be known, there would be no way that we would have known Him. He is so in a class by Himself that God needs to help us try to relate to who He is. He is so by Himself that there is nothing to compare Him to. He is not the most significant thing in a class; He is in a class all by Himself.

There are times in the Bible where He says, "I am kind of like the wind, but not really," "I am like fire, but I'm not fire," "I am like the rain, but I'm not rain." How about God is a tabernacle? A lamb, a ram, a dove, a priest, a prophet, a parable? How about this? Or that?

It is almost as though God is laboring in everything, working to get us to relate Him to something we can understand. Yet, He still wants us to know that when we think we have Him figured out, He is still not that!

God is saying, "What you have to know about Me is that I am holy. I am God. Whatever you can point to, I am not that. I am other than that. I am the creator, and you can know a little bit about me by studying creation, but don't get Me mixed up with creation because I am not creation. I am not a rock; I am not a bird, a plan, not part of the things I have created. I am other, holy, and above all else. I am not subject to the thing I have created. I can create something and make you subject to it, but I don't have to be subject to it."

Like a potter dealing with clay, He stands on the outside of the wheel and puts His hands on the clay, but He is never getting up on the wheel. God is not bound by gravity and time. He created laws of gravity, motion, and physics, but God is not bound by the rules He has created. God says He is above the law, so He will walk on water. He will defy gravity. You say 1+1=2? Give Him some fishes and loaves! It is appointed once unto man to die, but He will show you His resurrection power!

God is not bound by the laws He has created. If we are going to understand God, if we are going to get Him, if our faith is going to work, then we must start by understanding what God is not. God is not a man. He is not good, like we are good. His goodness is not like ours. His ways are not like our ways. His justice is not like our justice. When we don't understand God, we start to make Him like a god who is superhuman, as though God is a man with extraordinary characteristics and abilities.

But that is not God. Here is how it works: When God looked to His left nobody was there; when He looked to His right nobody was there. He is God all by Himself; nobody can compare, and nobody is in His category.

The Bible doesn't teach that God is smart; the Bible teaches that God knows all things. So, God doesn't learn or need to study something, gather statistics, or take counsel. God is not reasoning. He knows. He doesn't have to figure out your situation, and He isn't "working on it.".

He just knows that sparrow fell out of the tree, how many hairs are on your head, how and where the grass grows, the number of sands on the beach. God does not need information from you, and He doesn't learn; He knows everything. The Bible doesn't say that God is strong; it says that God has all the power. That means God works without using any effort. He doesn't have to get ready to do a miracle. He works without effort, and it doesn't take anything for God to do everything!

Jeremiah 32:27 says, *"Behold, I am the Lord, the God of all flesh. Is there anything too hard for me?"* The Bible says that God is not just everywhere, but He fills all things. He fills time and space. He doesn't go through time. He wasn't in your yesterday and then moving into your tomorrow. God stands at one time filling all your yesterday, today, and tomorrow at the same time.

I believe God desires to be worshipped by a creation that can wonder. God desires to be worshipped by a creature that has the capacity for awe. Man is the only creation that can experience wonder and awe. Birds don't sit in a tree and look at the sunset and say, "Wow!" A fish swims his whole life in the ocean and never says, "Man, this place is deep!" They don't have the capacity for such things.

God made a creature that can look everywhere and see the things He has made. Humans can see what He has done; they can stand in awe of creation. God does things to provoke wonder and awe.

You can get lost in anything God has made if you study the universe, DNA, outer space, your hand! He is so inexhaustible that no thumbprint is the same. Nothing He does has to be duplicated because He will never come to the end of what He is doing.

You can be amazed at what people get lost in; just watch Discovery or History channel! People study everything; the study of Pedology or dirt, Gerontology or aging and old age, Pomology or fruit growing, Oology, or bird eggs. Anything God has made has so many layers to it that you can get lost in it. God wants us to know that He is this awesome and this wonderful; He did all this, and He wants us to be in awe of Him!

When we lose our wonder of who God is, we make God our tiny pocket Jesus idol. He is no different than an idol on a hill, a genie in a magical bottle, or a source of wishes. Tell your mountain about your God! Whatever you are dealing with and going through, physically, emotionally, or spiritually, God is bigger than anything!

"I lift my eyes to the hills, from where does my help come from? My help comes from the Lord – maker of heaven and earth." Where once David would say this while looking to a mountain of idols, high above where he stood in a valley, we now look to the same hill, which God redeemed,

and know that the Creator of Heaven and earth, hung on a hill. On a mountain top, he redeemed all of creation. He conquered even the high places, even the idols, the ideology of man. He cannot compare.

Job 26:14,

"Behold, these are but the outskirts of His ways, and how small a whisper do we hear of Him! But the thunder of His power who can understand?"

Isaiah 40:28,

"Have you not known? Have you not heard? The Lord is the everlasting God, the Creator of the ends of the earth. He does not faint or grow weary; His understanding is unsearchable."

Psalm 8:3-4,

"When I look at Your heavens, the work of Your fingers, the moon and the stars, which You have set in place, what is man that You are mindful of him, and the son of man that You care for Him?"

Tell your mountain about your God.

CONNECT

WITH SUSANNE RYAN

SusanneRyan.com

(Sermons online, artwork, and more!)

 SRyanS

 SusanneRyan

 info@susanneryan.com

PURCHASE ONLINE @ AMAZON!

HOLY SHEEP: *A devotional with a little bit of humor and a lot of inspiration.*

By Susanne M Ryan

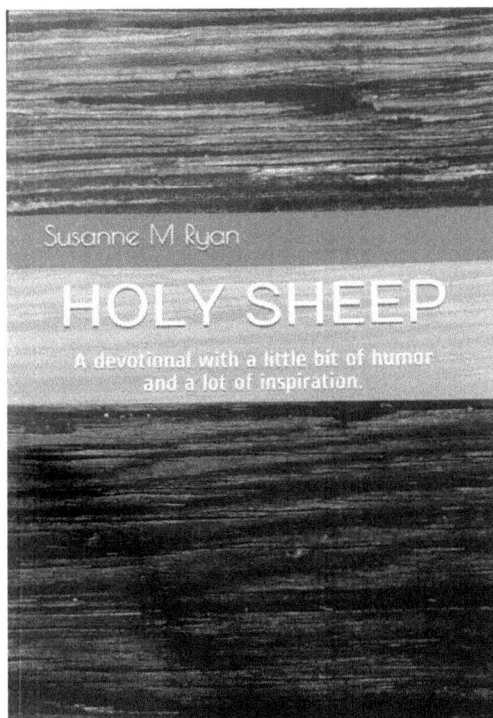

COVER ME IN TIMES OF WAR

PURCHASE ONLINE @ AMAZON!

POCKET JESUS: *Making Jesus Big*

By Susanne M Ryan

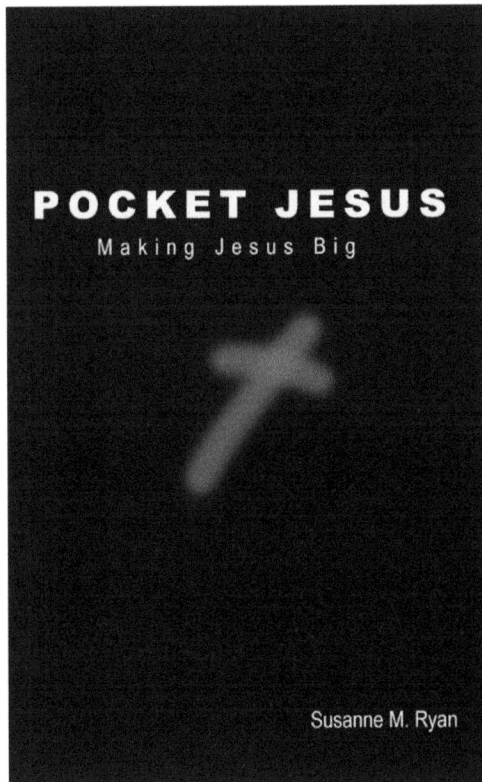

Are you looking for a good church?

ABOUT THE AUTHOR

Susanne grew up in Hemet, California. She is the youngest daughter of Pastors Bob & Susan Beckett, of the DP City Church. Susanne has been married to Steve since 2001. Both Steve and Susanne have been in ministry for many years, and between the two of them have ministered in every area on the church campus. They were youth pastors for over five years and saw the youth ministry grow from 20 kids to over 125 kids per week. Their motto in youth ministry was "Church for those who hate church," and they welcomed kids from all backgrounds – church youth to street youth.

Susanne has the heart to preach the Word of God in a way that will reach inside a church building as well as outside on the streets. She has been known to bring a sense of humor along with pure Biblical truths when preaching the Gospel.

Susanne is currently the leader of Chosen Chicks Women's Ministry at DP City Church. She is also the vice-principal at the church's Christian School, DP Christian School. She has currently written two other books, 'Pocket Jesus' and 'Holy Sheep.'

Susanne and Steve live in Hemet, California, and together they have two girls, Sierra and Cheyenne.

You can contact Susanne at info@susanneryan.com.

9 780578 769004